BECOME
YOUR OWN
BUSINESS
GURU

TESTIMONIALS

"Powerful! Wisdom filled! Practical! *Become Your Own Business Guru* offers a compelling model for the way we think of wealth, our relationship to abundance, and the role it plays in our lives. Through personal stories and true-life accounts, life-coach strategist Gary Quinn reveals how ordinary events of life offer an extraordinary window to our inner dialogue of abundance and sense of worth. Once we recognize this relationship, the path to spiritual, as well as material, abundance in our lives becomes obvious. By sharing the powerful revelations from his own experience, Gary offers practical templates that we can apply in our lives to healing, business, and relationships. Whether you're an artist or an engineer, a homemaker, or a policymaker, this book is about you, your life, and every relationship that you'll ever experience. *Become Your Own Business Guru* should be required reading for everyone who has ever felt like there's something missing in the mainstream view of what's possible for us in the world. *Become Your Own Business Guru* catapults us beyond the obvious, showing us that our ability to receive is directly linked to our courage to love ourselves. I love this book!"
— Gregg Braden, scientist and *New York Times* bestselling author of *The Wisdom Codes and the Divine Matrix*

"Gary has written a comprehensive guide to creating balance and awareness in your business from a practical yet spiritual perspective. Thank you, Gary, for helping make the spiritual laws actionable in real life and business!"
— Mariel Hemingway, Academy Award–nominated actress and health activist

"Gary Quinn's new book *Become Your Own Business Guru* is a fresh exploration of how individuals can develop new positive techniques, identify and change beliefs, and create a conscious self in business."
—David Bailey CEO, The Bailey Group

"This book is a gift—a reminder of how gratitude, attitude, authenticity, and of course love is so important in our lives. Thank you Gary, this will be a great help in guiding us to navigate these times, which can be challenging for us all."
—Belinda Carlisle, international recording artist, singer, *New York Times* bestselling author, and co-founder of Animals People Alliance

"Gary Quinn is the perfect person to write this important book. *Become Your Own Business Guru* is a transformative handbook providing guidance, vision, and a new way of looking at your relationship with the business world. Highly recommended."
—James F. Twyman, *New York Times* bestselling author and Peace Troubadour

"Gary has the precious gift to be clear and straight! It's time to change, and this manual investigates all the possible ways to do it successfully. It's complete, simple to adopt, and very understandable! Thank you, Gary, for generously sharing your heart and mind with us."
—Katia Da Ros, vice president, Irinox SpA, Italy

"Gary is a truly inspirational, kind, and generous human being. He is a master of his craft, helping people realize their life dreams, and his new book is a blueprint to your success."
—David Courtney, Grammy-nominated songwriter, music producer, and author

"I have known Gary Quinn for more than twenty-five years. His leadership and problem-solving skills make Gary Quinn an expert in business relationships. These characteristics are defined and showcased beautifully in his latest work, *Become Your Own Business Guru*. Gary helps anyone feel better about the work they do, and I highly recommend reading his book to enhance your business today."

—Scott Savlov, CEO and executive producer at Savlov Consulting Sports and Entertainment TV

"In a timely intervention, Gary's methodology opens the door to a new self-understanding, required to meet the challenges of today's era of noise and data overload. Activating the affirmative life force that resides within us all, his practices lead us to listen, learn, and grow. Business leaders will do well to accept the invitation and join the conversation."

—Ray Keane, PE founding principal at Engineering 350, LEED® AP

"*Become Your Own Business Guru* is an adjustment for the soul. In his book, Gary shares great advice and techniques for how one can take control of their thinking and live in a more fulfilling way by just being authentic."

—Arturo Cisneros, artist management, PSA Entertainment, LLC

"Gary has always known how to help quiet our minds and keep the flow of positivity. His narrative of light, awareness, and knowledge keeps us on our toes while providing us with the tools we need to be as successful. Anything is truly possible when we come from the space that *all things are possible*. I am blessed for our twenty-five years of friendship and for this helpful guide to success."

—Gena Lee Nolin, actor, bestselling author, health advocate, and founder of *Thyroid Sexy*

"Gary has a unique insight that can pierce right through the mind's clutter and inspire the strong conviction of "I can do this." Often, we are the primary obstacle, in our own way of reaching our dreams. Gary can not only see these obstacles but can see the solutions, and he also has the skills to help us create a new path for success and happiness. That journey has a lovely way of igniting joy in us and others in our workplaces and elsewhere, which is a giant bonus. Thank you, Gary, for helping us find a more compassionate way to succeed in business and in life. Such a needed formula in our world."
  —Cozette Dunlap, president, D. D. Dunlap
  Companies, Inc.

"This book left me feeling recharged and ready to take my business to the next level. As a young entrepreneur, this information is invaluable."
  —Lana Johnson, designer and president, Orseund Iris

"Gary's coaching over the years has taken me and my luxury real estate business well beyond where I ever could have imagined I would be. His new book, *Become Your Own Business Guru*, gives us a clear blueprint for inspirational business growth, self-awareness, and change."
  —Debra Johnston, global luxury specialist, Coldwell
  Banker Realty

"This book combines practical wisdom with pure magic, making the reader feel a definitive shift after a few short chapters. Improve your business and any other area of your life with this impactful guide. Thank you, Gary, for another masterpiece!"
  —Linda Kelley, cofounder, Indigo Payments

"Gary Quinn is a master at bringing an authentic, centered approach to building an abundant life and business. He provides essential knowledge and easy suggestions on how to tap into and activate the power and knowledge you have within. This book is essential not only in your business plan but in your *life* plan."

—Hanna Bolte, SVP marketing/communications/talent, Estrella Media Television

"Gary has no shortage of remarkable ideas, and he has the will to execute them. He is a joyous person who abounds with energy because he is functioning at a higher frequency. I owe my success to having listened respectfully to Gary's best advice and allowing him to transform my life. Gary cultivates the habits of happiness, and he attracts people and situations that match his frequency. For all readers, *Become Your Own Business Guru* is my choice today."

—Sante Losio, founder/CEO, Longevitime.com

"As you become more successful in business, worries, anxieties, and uncertainties creep in, disrupting your vision, energy, flow, and inspiration. It's easy to lose your way, miss important signposts, and ultimately fail. Fortunately, Gary Quinn has created the formula for long-term success in both your business and your personal life with his latest book, *Become Your Own Business Guru*. It's a must-read for all aspiring business leaders."

—Ilyce R. Glink, author, founder and CEO of Best Money Moves

"*Become Your Own Business Guru* helps us form positive habits, master our consciousness, and achieve professional success. Gary gives us a path to become our best selves."

—Victoria Cordova, writer, producer, and director

"This book is a breath of much-needed fresh air in a time of creative evolution. Gary Quinn gives solid advice and is one of the most innovative business and life coaches of our time. He helps you take the next *big step* toward creating extraordinary results."
　　—Laurie D. Muslow, creative strategist and CEO of It's All Good Entertainment

"Gary is truly a master at helping others realize their dreams and empowering them to activate their potential. In his new book, *Become Your Own Business Guru*, Gary skillfully and divinely illuminates strategic keys that will help open major doors for business leaders looking to elevate themselves."
　　—Dr. Landon McCarroll, CEO and president, DermKing Institute

"*Become Your Own Business Guru* guides you to follow your own inner path to self-fulfillment and harness your spiritual intelligence, thus creating positive business methods to reach your personal goals. A wonderfully informative book!"
　　—Anita Moorjani, *New York Times* bestselling author of *Dying to be Me*

"Gary Quinn's new book *Become Your Own Business Guru* offers magnificent tools to gain self-esteem and self-appreciation, and best of all, a sense of being a productive, successful, and happy person."
　　—Dara Torres, five-time Olympic champion, twelve-time Olympic medalist, *New York Times* bestselling author, fitness advocate, and motivational speaker

"*Become Your Own Business Guru* is filled with tools you can use to release your limitations and transform your life. This empowering book is a must-read for anyone seeking to become more self-aware."
   —Bob Hurwitz, founder and CEO, Hurwitz James Company

"An inspirational and informative resource on awakening dreams, attaining balance, and attracting abundance! Innovative life coach Gary Quinn guides us on a journey to achieve our dreams and goals in his comprehensive new book, *Become Your Own Business Guru*."
   —Sherrod Taylor, actor and writer

"One of the many strategies Gary offers in his new book is to use beautiful memories to elevate your present emotional state. Among my treasured memories is having high tea in London with this magic man who lives and breathes everything he teaches."
   —Pam Grout, author of twenty books, including *New York Times* number-one bestsellers

"Influential, powerful, and inspirational in every aspect. In *Become Your Own Business Guru*, Gary Quinn takes us on the journey of how to make every moment in our life count, to be thankful, and how living is all about healing and creating balance in our life. Thank you, Gary, for your inspiration and this masterpiece."
   —Maryam Morrison, founder and editor-in-chief of *The Eden* magazine

"*Become Your Own Business Guru* helps you become a master of relationships by teaching you how to commit to letting go of old behaviors and fear-based patterns. This book is essential for those working to find happiness and authenticity."

—Judson Rothschild, CEO of Rothschild Interiors and author of *Snap Out of It?*

"Gary's new book is a wonderful tool that you can use to gain inner clarity and manifest your fondest desires. At the end of the day, the money you make isn't a true measure of your success, but rather wealth is just a byproduct of the process. Instead, it is the feeling of fulfillment and peace of mind that will make you feel abundantly rich and happy. For me, Gary's book is a wonderful reminder that if you can envision a goal and believe in yourself to achieve it, then you are certain to accomplish anything you put your mind to."

—Nick Wilder, international actor, author, and musician

GARY QUINN

BECOME YOUR OWN BUSINESS GURU

Create a Balanced Path to Well-Being,
Success, and Happiness

ARCHWAY
PUBLISHING

Archway Publishing books may be ordered through booksellers or by contacting:

Archway Publishing
1663 Liberty Drive
Bloomington, IN 47403
www.archwaypublishing.com
844-669-3957

ISBN: 978-1-6657-2312-1 (sc)
ISBN: 978-1-6657-2310-7 (hc)
ISBN: 978-1-6657-2311-4 (e)

Library of Congress Control Number: 2022908316

Print information available on the last page.

Archway Publishing rev. date: 7/5/2022

You are the creator of your dreams. You are the pathfinder who, with courage and desire, will seek to discover the key to your personal success.

—Gary Quinn

CONTENTS

INTRODUCTION

Each decade presents new challenges and opportunities in all different aspects of the workforce. Some people are finding their way to the top of newly emerging fields, while others are seeing their typical work environment change drastically and unexpectedly. Sometimes, our economy is not quite ready for such drastic changes, causing much unrest and uncertainty for companies and employees alike. When the future is unpredictable or concerning, you must look within yourself and focus your attention there. Positive changes come quickly when your inner and outer worlds align with your goals and desires. Ideas, thoughts, and feelings take form in matter. Therefore, if you want something to take place in the outer, tangible world, you must first have the mental component of a blueprint for success.

Throughout history, countless epidemics and disasters have shaken the foundation of society. These difficult situations have been impactful and changed the way that generations of people live their daily lives. However, the importance of forming positive business habits in even the most challenging of situations, such as during a pandemic or an economic recession, often goes overlooked.

Millions are living longer, better lives than ever before, and everyone has access to greater levels of performance and achievement anyone. Yet most people have never learned the proven self-empowerment tools and time-tested strategies that form the basis for business success. You are the creator of your dreams. You are the pathfinder who, with courage and desire, seeks to discover the key to your success. You are not merely the sum of your material possessions, your work, or your achievements. You are not a "human doing"; you are a "human being."

Everyone faces hardships and barriers to their success. You cannot avoid the hard work needed to achieve your goals. All you can do is have discipline, implement repetition, and restructure your belief system. It all starts with you. As you begin to modify your thoughts, words, and actions, you start to change the way you feel about yourself. Your life is directed by your choices. This business handbook will teach you how to become more conscious of creating these choices, leading you out of the fear and confusion in which most people live. You will learn how to find balance and have a breakthrough in your life.

This unique handbook addresses these critical avenues and encourages us to make healthy lifestyle changes that will balance our lives and enable a blueprint for lasting success. You will walk away knowing how to take 100 percent responsibility for your thoughts and make changes that will have a lifelong impact on your professional and personal life. The business world can be daunting, so I have decided to cover the topics most relevant to our collective human struggles while being concise enough so exceptionally active individuals have enough time to pick up this handbook.

This business handbook teaches you how to reprogram your daily thoughts and actions with exercises focused on changing your belief system through awareness and acceptance of change. The daily empowerment affirmations in this handbook are statements that will help you activate the change within yourself. A proven model of success is to take action steps each day toward achieving any goal and to enhance your unique abilities by using NLP, meditation, yoga, affirmations, and stress-reducing mind techniques. The goal is to create a calmer, more centered, and more balanced person, with reduced fear and anxiety.

It is critical to use the power of intent to fulfill your desires and manifest self-confidence and self-love. You must follow a principal strategy of bringing your most impressive self into the workplace. Conscious thinking patterns, regular exercise (done with the power of intention), and daily meditation are the three cornerstones of balancing your mind, body, and work. While I suggest you closely follow the thought and speech patterns, exercises, and information about meditation I have chosen to share with you, remember, you won't wake up a rigid purist. We live in the real world. All you need do is make mindful, conscious choices and understand the personal power you possess. As you understand the power of decision-making, you will welcome more positive experiences, people, and opportunities into your life. As we become more authentic, we look better and feel better. As our energy flows, we glow.

It takes twenty-one days to train ourselves to adapt to changes, and some of these changes may be drastic for many of you. However, I urge you not to give up. As you persist and succeed, you will feel a carefreeness that you may not have felt since you were a young child. Your body will respond on a cellular level to the positive new thoughts, energies, and exercises you are feeding it. Your mind will be quieted, and there will be clarity and a sense of calm, which you may have once thought impossible to attain. We all need to accept that we are part of the grand scheme of life and that universal laws apply to our bodies, our spirits, our minds, and our souls. *Become Your Own Business Guru* will guide you and enable you to reconnect with the positive energy that naturally flows through the universe. This energy is infinitely accessible to everyone at any time. However, we must be willing and teachable. It is up to you to take action, and you can start right now, by investing your time into this business handbook, which has gravitated to you because you were seeking out a manual for your success. I have faith that *Become Your Own Business Guru* will be a source of inspiration and knowledge and well help you each day to bring your complete and authentic self to the workplace.

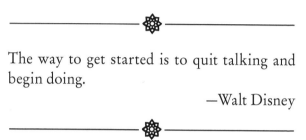

The way to get started is to quit talking and begin doing.

—Walt Disney

CHAPTER

1

❋

WAITING FOR HAPPINESS

The world is ever-changing, and how we interact with one another personally and professionally is no exception. We must now reinvent, restart, and revive ourselves and our strategies to create new results in the business world. Especially in the professional world, it's easy to get stuck in the same old patterns and fall into comfortable routines. Workers expect stability, and employers expect their workers to be consistent. However, the startling reality is that the business world changes rapidly and mercilessly, and those who don't adapt are left behind. When any global crisis takes hold, businesses and individuals must keep up with ever-changing technology and expectations.

The definition of "company culture" has quickly evolved. For a long time, it was generally accepted that people just needed to show up and do their jobs to be successful. In the modern era, employees want to be somewhere where they can be highly engaged, build a network, and contribute to a purpose-driven business. These qualities are no longer mere incentives for company; in our rapidly changing world, they are becoming requirements to retain top employees and stay relevant. Both corporations and individuals must adapt and innovate or fall behind the curve and be left in the dust, wondering where things went wrong.

For any business or company, no matter the size, to upgrade to the next level, it must start with the individual. Which means *you*. After all, professional growth is not possible without personal growth. There are four simple steps you can follow today, starting this moment, to change yourself for the better.

The first step is to activate self-belief within yourself. This is the number-one rule, because if you don't believe in yourself, then who will? There are already many obstacles in life, so you don't need to limit your potential by worrying and saying, "Is it possible?"

The second step is to define your vision. You need a clear picture in your mind of what you want. Each great achievement results from time and energy devoted toward a concise goal.

The third step is to set challenging goals for yourself or your business. It may seem daunting at first, but good things in life don't often come easily. If your goal is worth striving toward, you will be more content and accomplished when you reach it. Keep in mind that you *will* reach your goals; it's only a matter of time and effort.

The fourth and final step is to create a plan of action or a blueprint for success. This will be your guiding light that you can fall back on whenever you're unsure of the path ahead.

The combination of these four steps is a simple but timeless method you can use to start taking action and transforming into the person you've always dreamed of becoming.

BUSINESS KEY CODE

Changing a reality can be a conscious choice, selected at will by a person, or it can be an unconscious choice based on an intended desire.

COMMUNICATION

Working in the business world means you must communicate about all the services and products that make you or your company stand out. One of the first rules to success is to let people know what you have to offer and why they need it. Often, people hide what they have to offer. They even conceal themselves from the world, and then they wonder why their business ventures aren't returning enough wealth to sustain their finances. It's not enough anymore to know marketing principles or business fundamentals. New digital platforms are emerging daily, and the people who can't alter their approach to business will continue to struggle. If you patiently observe the professional world, you will find some of the largest companies in the world communicate what they have to offer to the public constantly and consistently. They know the value of keeping their name, product, and service in front of the public eye. From now until the day you retire, pay close attention to how you communicate with your customers and clients. Always make sure they are fully aware of what makes you the best and why they can't afford to go another day without you taking care of their needs.

It's important to be a good communicator. The most

successful people know how to broadcast their ideas so that other people can understand and grasp. Successful people are able to communicate their talents and their abilities and share openly. It is time to start opening your awareness and communicating in a healthy and empowering way. You must learn to listen to others to build trust so they will share their honest desires, goals, and dreams. The greatest gift you can give another human being is to accept his or her communication and receive it without passing judgment. Don't take it personally when the truth isn't pleasant, especially when it comes from the people closest to you. Remember: if you can't endure the truth, others won't want to speak it to you.

One of our impediments to progress is treating communication like a one-way street, when in reality, it is a mutual concession. There is a give-and-take in each conversation, and you must take total responsibility for the outcome of each exchange. You must communicate with a clear intention and a distinct image in mind of the expected result. The real challenge lies in taking full responsibility for the other individual who is receiving and internalizing your communication. Being in full control of what you advertise to others means being completely in touch with yourself and your subconsciousness so you approach any exchange with a clear and honest intent. What we don't intend to communicate about ourselves can take over and speak louder than our words if we are not always living as our authentic selves.

Often, we communicate nonverbally, and we use our words to hide what we truly feel and desire. As children, we learned that if we spoke out of turn or asked the wrong question, we could be punished or sent to our rooms without dinner. Remember, you have a precious soul within you, and it is your responsibility to take care of this soul, heal it, and never again suppress any of these profound feelings. You are now a mature human being, and you have a right to communicate your feelings with the voice of an adult, not that of a dependent child. If you do not address this changing dynamic, you will create those same negative situations and conditions you faced or experienced as a child. If you are truthful and let your authentic self's voice speak, you will discover you have tremendous newfound freedom and a foundation for self-expression that will last a lifetime.

MINDFULNESS

Many define mindfulness a mentality or habit of paying close attention to one's own actions. In reality, it's a tool that, when used wisely, can boost your experience at work, your relationships with others, and even your overall well-being. Mindfulness is maintaining moment-to-moment awareness of your thoughts, feelings, and emotions while having an attitude of kindness and curiosity. Mindfulness has a direct impact on your work culture and team effectiveness. Being mindful of your sense of safety can boost everyone around you at work. When team members feel safe and trust one another, they feel more accomplished and do more. Mindfulness starts with making a mental commitment to it. Mindfulness is an important tool that can raise self-awareness and help you identify important needs more clearly, building an intention for your practice before you jump in.

READY, SET, TAKE ACTION

It can be challenging to find a moment and location to follow through with these exercises. You may want to wake up thirty minutes earlier than usual to allow yourself time each day to devote to practicing mindfulness.

1. Find a comforting, calming location. It can be indoors or outdoors; it need only be a soothing location. Turn off your mobile phone. Leave your possessions behind when you access this healing site.

2. Shut your eyes and relax. Be aware of all the sounds around you. Direct your awareness toward all sounds, nearby and distant. Take a deep breath, and slowly turn your attention toward nothing but your own breathing.

3. Inhale slowly, holding your breath for a count of six seconds. Then, as you let out your breath, release all your negative energy and fear. Now inhale again, slowly, while visualizing the air flowing into your body and filling your lungs. If you find yourself losing focus, don't shut down. Just recognize that your attention is wandering, then take the time to redirect your energy back to your breathing.

4. Repeat this mindful breathing for at least two or three minutes. Continue training your breathing, and with time, you'll find it becomes easier. It is a powerful technique that you can use anywhere throughout your day.

It is crucial to share your feelings, needs, and ideas in a genuine way will attract good people who see your value and want to grow with you. There are two ways to communicate: an empowering way and a disempowering way. Unfortunately, society has taught us since youth to communicate in a disempowering way, by blaming other people for the information or knowledge we feel we lack. You must take responsibility for your feelings and actions. In the Far East, this is called Karma. Essentially, karma is the result of a person's actions as well as the outcomes of these actions. It is a matter of cause and effect. Here in the West, we call it the law of reciprocity. What you give, you get back. Just as gravity is a law of the physical world, so is Karma a law of the metaphysical world. We are held responsible for the intention of all our actions, and the energy we have right now is the result of yesterday's karma.

Taking care of your body is equally important. The old adage admonishes you to "treat your body like a temple." Why? What's the connection between a temple and the physical manifestation of our human existence? Let's enter a temple and gather more information.

A temple is a site that inspires reverence. When we enter a temple, we are filled with the presence of something bigger and more powerful than ourselves. We may kneel or genuflect, fold our hands in prayer, or sit in devout silence, but our behavior is always respectful, caring, and attentive as we acknowledge this entity. Whatever nomenclature we use to describe this phenomenon, we feel the presence of something greater than we could have imagined. At the same time, we understand we are not separate from this presence. We are connected to it in powerful ways, dependent on it, and humbled by it. We are strengthened by the recognition of this need for spiritual attachment.

We are both physical and metaphysical beings. All spiritual practices address the nature of our existence, the duality of our bodies and our spirits. We cannot properly take care of our physical form without taking care of our metaphysical well-being. The two fragments of the complete human are inextricably intertwined. When our bodies become toxic from work-related stress, self-doubt, poor nutrition, or lack of exercise, both our bodies and spirits become depleted. It is necessary we take time for ourselves. We require quiet, meditative time to go within ourselves and let go of the stress. By doing this, we manifest peace and healing within.

When we eat heavily processed foods, typically laden with fat and sugar, we do more than make ourselves lethargic, overweight, and unattractive. Our soul and spirit are affected just as much as our bodies. We feel awful, not just because we've eaten food that is not nourishing our bodies (our temples) but also because we are not providing our spirit and soul with the correct nutrition. The more we neglect our long-term health, the more we become alienated from our metaphysical growth.

So many of us neglect and abuse our bodies because we're overtired, overworked, overly stressed, and overburdened with responsibilities. Positive thinking, proper exercise, and meditation are ways in which we honor, preserve, and respect our temple. These actions also allow our highest level of energy to guide us through every moment of the day. Thereby, we become focused and clear about our purpose—in our careers and our lives. In addition, this newfound vitality will, of course, change how we function in our work environment.

Let's be clear about stress. We all need a certain amount of it in our lives, or we would never again use our brains. There is no way to live stress-free lives, nor should we. The normal stress of daily life and work can inspire us to be creative, reach out to others, and participate fully in life. It can keep us alert to danger, help us find innovative solutions, and make us feel like integral parts of our workplace and community. The danger comes when we allow our lives to become so overstressed that practically every minute of the day, we must deal with pressing problems until we feel like screaming. Some of us withdraw into depression, while others distract ourselves by overeating or loading up on coffee. Some drink too much alcohol or drown out their real feelings using prescription medication. Others spend countless hours at the computer, living fantasy lives online. We shop online, check social media, or sit for hours in front of the television, remote in hand, so we don't have to face the chaos that has crept into our lives and overwhelmed us. We all try to escape in our own way.

The hard truth is that when there is too much stress, there is no escape. The individual's system of avoidance starts to break down and eventually, it gives way. The structure that holds together the temple becomes shaky, unreliable, and worst of all, unsafe. Our bodies deteriorate as we become increasingly alienated from the true yearnings of our spiritual nature. The elusive solution is simply to stop causing ourselves unnecessary stress. Accept the stress you can't avoid, embrace it, and grow from it, but don't bite off more than you can chew. The modern human has an unfortunate habit of causing themselves unnecessary problems. We must no longer stand in the way of our own progress; instead, we must devote the entirety of our energy to conquering the problems in our path and fortifying our temple.

BUSINESS KEY CODE

Change the thought, and take the proper action necessary to love yourself and your body, which is your temple.

EXERCISE AND ATTITUDE

Fitness and exercise clubs report that their membership ranks swell dramatically in early January, at the end of the traditional heavy eating period between November and New Year. But all too soon, many of these new fitness enthusiasts, who were so eager to get into shape on January 1, end up working out sporadically or dropping out completely. New Year's resolutions are fleeting, but self-discipline and follow-through are central to a successful attitude. While we make these promises with good intentions, interestingly, we often lack the power of intention, which is simply harnessing the energy that fuels the desire for change and performing the new action consistently. If we exercise only because of guilt or because we've made a financial commitment, we are not working from the power of intention. If we work out at a fitness facility, go hiking, ride a bike, do yoga, or take a lap in the swimming pool, we work our bodies with the intention of raising our energy level, toning our muscles, and feeling good about ourselves. We just have to do it mindfully and consistently, without ever dropping out.

The modern world deluges us with constant data. The Internet, television, personal indication devices—all the technology that supports and aids us—can also overwhelm us and keep us in a constant state of stress. Where's the next text or email? Who can I call now? What can I ask Siri? What can I find scrolling through Instagram and LinkedIn? What music can I listen to? What Netflix show can distract me? We cannot simply be at peace with ourselves—simply *be*. We forget how to connect with the spiritual power that feeds and fuels us, understanding we are part of something incomprehensible that is larger than ourselves and more intricate than our high-tech toys.

To create the *Become Your Own Business Guru* attitude, action is critical. When you're walking through life in a state of positive energy, it acts as a powerful magnet that will attract the right people and opportunities to elevate you. When those people and opportunities finally appear, you must take the time to integrate them into your plan for achieving your goals and well-being. Changing your life can be as simple as changing your mind. We all make mistakes. Life is like a classroom, where learning from your errors is much more valuable than clinging to the past. Now is your time to regain your personal power and surge toward happiness and success.

DAILY EMPOWERMENT AFFIRMATION

Everything in life is here for me to have exactly what I want!

THE WRAP-UP: ALL YOU NEED TO KNOW

- ❀ Commit to you as a success, acknowledge those around you, and think of ways to make your clients feel special.
- ❀ Create a blueprint for success so you always have a plan to fall back on when times get tough.
- ❀ Learn how to listen to others so they will share their honest desires, goals, and dreams.
- ❀ Communicate with those you love, as well as all your clients and relationships.
- ❀ Show your appreciation and give something to those who are giving to you or using your services.
- ❀ You *will* reach your goals as long as you put in the time and effort.
- ❀ Genuinely share your feelings, needs, and ideas so you attract people into your life who appreciate your value.
- ❀ Have a good posture, dress impeccably, be well-groomed, and always look prosperous and confident.

2

❁

NLP: HAVE A BREAKTHROUGH, NOT A BREAKDOWN

Neurolinguistic programming is a therapeutic method created to educate people about self-awareness and effective communication. NLP can be used to model and change patterns of mental and emotional behavior. Our thought processes are so powerful, they can influence our energy, our body language, and therefore, our ability to achieve our goals. It's only logical we explore how we can influence the way we think to better ourselves and strive for balance in our lives.

Let's go back in time, to the University of Santa Cruz. In 1972, Assistant Linguistics Professor John Grinder and senior Psychology student Richard Bandler collaborated on revolutionary research about achieving "excellence." The study of thought patterns and how they affect our reality was a new frontier for some, with many accomplished therapists of the time creating their own techniques to harness this dormant energy. John and Richard set out to gather and refine these methods, and four years later, neurolinguistic programming was born. This discipline can show you how to reprogram your neurological processes and your language so you can set out to achieve any goal you set for yourself.

NLP is a vast subject, with plenty of interesting readings I'd like to suggest (check the reading list at the end of the handbook). However, for the sake of this handbook, we will focus on NLP's most important concepts and principles, which you can use in your daily life to *Become Your Own Business Guru.*

BUSINESS KEY CODE

Continue to raise your frequency through your thoughts and words to reflect what you choose to attract in this life.

Let's start with the first letter in NLP, which stands for *neuro.* This refers to our five senses (sight, hearing, smell, taste, touch). These senses dictate the way we experience the world around us, and they give our brains a way to comprehend our surroundings. Scientists estimate that every passing second, about 2 million bits of data are available for our senses to detect. Out of those 2 million, we can process a mere 126 bits, which means it's up to our minds to choose what tiny bits of information will enter our consciousness. The key question is this: Out of those 2 million bits, are you picking the best 126 that you can? As it turns out, the part of our brain in charge of picking these 126 bits, dubbed the RAS (reticular activating system), can be trained to better align with our conscious goals and objectives. To try this yourself, begin by keeping a clear and vivid objective in mind, such as growing your career or getting a promotion. To make this goal as attainable as possible, you must employ visualizations, specifically by imagining how your senses would respond to your success.

For example: What would you see when you achieved your goal? How would that accomplishment feel for you and for the other people involved in it? What would that sound like? Would there be a particular smell or emotion? After visualizing, your RAS will pass the information from the conscious part of the brain to the subconscious part. As we take action and our new reality starts to form, our subconsciousness detects that we are aligning with our visualizations and pushes us to take conscious action in our day-to-day lives that will bring us closer to our goals.

Life is full of causes and effects, and NLP helps us to differentiate between a lifestyle of cause and one of effect. Living at cause fundamentally means acting with the knowledge that you are in control of your choices, that you always decide how to react and behave to the people and events you experience every day. It also means you take responsibility for every choice that you make, no matter the outcome. Almost everybody is living at cause when they make a decision and get the outcome they want, because that is not so hard to do. What is difficult, what requires constant work and discipline, is living in a state of cause even when you fail.

In a corporate setting, it behooves anyone to know each department head and the individuals within those departments. In this way, employees better understand the systems and strategies used, thereby allowing for upward movement within the company ranks. You must operate at a frequency of high energy to connect with people in specific areas of a corporation. For example, let's say you're in the real estate world and you desire to be the top-grossing agent in your area. To accomplish this, you must have market knowledge, a large client base, and the confidence and competence to present a home. After closing a deal successfully, it becomes easy to take responsibility for the triumph and claim you achieved your goals because you prepared and strategized. If, on the other hand, the deal slipped through your fingers, it would be much harder to take full responsibility for the outcome and your unsuccessful approach. After a bad outcome, people are far more likely to say things like, "The deal could never have worked out" and "They would never consider me for the position." These excuses do not represent what living at cause truly means, and even though some of those ramifications may be true, they do not help you improve in the long run.

Each of us has a choice to live through each moment "at cause" or "at effect." You must try to live every moment of your life "at cause" if you want to own up to your errors and create future success. To accomplish this, it helps to follow a NLP assumption: there is no failure, only feedback. While living this way is difficult and requires a good amount of fortitude, it is incredibly empowering to feel and act in full control over your life. The alternative is to live "at effect," which represents blamelessly escaping from difficulties and responsibilities. It is incredibly disempowering to believe that the outcomes you receive, as well as your attitude and your day-to-day experiences, are the result of other people and events outside your control. This belief gives others an excessive amount of power over your life. By giving away your power, you will soon find yourself depending on others to feel powerful and successful. This dependency is not only limiting but can also cause great suffering.

No one can dictate how we feel, and no one can force us into action. Rather, we react to other people's behaviors the way we choose to react, and we take action of our own volition. Embracing the "at cause" lifestyle does not involve excluding other peoples' opinions from your decision-making process. It is often useful to ask friends for guidance and support. However, doing so requires taking conscious ownership of the decisions you make, the attitudes you display, and the results you get.

This exercise was created to help you become more aware of the subconscious habits that seep into everyday conversations. By becoming mindful of these habits, we can start to alter them if we believe they are obstacles to our authentic communication.

READY, SET, TAKE ACTION

In many business environments, defensiveness is a typical source of miscommunication and even conflict. We're not usually prepared to hear criticism, let alone grow from it, especially when it's given in a cold or rude way. This exercise introduces "I" statements, which will be used to describe others' actions while also giving the speaker the chance to share their perspective.

1. You can do this by yourself or with a coworker. Either way, you will need to take out a piece of paper and write down some scenarios where coworkers have lashed out at each other over disagreements, contracts, clients, or information that was withheld or falsified.
2. By yourself or with a coworker, create "I" statements regarding how the scenarios on the paper make you feel.
3. When disagreements within the company happen, you can't play the game of "right" or "wrong." You must be

a team player, negotiator, and problem solver instead of problem creator. The "I" statements allow you to share your perspective in a helpful way rather than a critical one.

4. In your communication, actions speak louder than words. People will be aware of your actions and will remember small courtesies. Your ability to communicate your feelings and your intention to resolve conflict will be noticed. It's important to know something personal about your coworkers, clients, or anybody with whom you do business. It only takes a few minutes, but the investment of time and attention can bring you great rewards.

Let us now discuss the second keyword in NLP: linguistic. Language is an essential element of our lives, yet we rarely take the time to reflect on how we use it and experience it. In the realm of NLP, language can be described as the process of communicating ideas to another person as well as to yourself. The first action step that every good communicator should take is to build rapport. It's simple to tell when two people are in rapport with each other, because they have similar body language, language patterns, and even breathing patterns. They are basically just "dancing to the same tune." Many couples who have been together for long enough will inevitably be in rapport, even in the minutia of their daily lives. Often in team sports, players on the same team will be in rapport, as will therapists who get to know their clients very well. Rapport is everywhere around. The first thing you need to do is notice it. Once you are able to observe rapport, you can begin to practice it. To match another person's vibe or energy, it is often easier to match their body language, followed by their verbal inflections and vocabulary. To be clear, matching another person's body language doesn't mean copying or mimicking it; it is much more subtle than that. It means matching body-weight distribution, posture, stance, and so on. What's important is that the imitation be as inconspicuous, noninvasive, and unexaggerated as possible. Otherwise, you might end up making a fool of yourself or even offending the other person. Voice-matching another person means matching the rhythm, volume, and tonality of their speech. When trying to voice-match with another person, first determine what representational system that person is using.

Each of our five senses represents a filter through which we experience the world, and each of them can also be called a representational system in NLP. Every single person uses all five of them, however we tend to use one system more than the others, and that is what we refer to as the primary representational system. Oftentimes people will either use a primary visual system, a primary auditory system, or a primary kinesthetic system. A primarily visual person will tend to use sight to experience the world more than anything else, while a person who is primarily auditory will use listening and a person who is primarily kinesthetic will use touch. A person's primary representational system will often influence their speech and behavior patterns. Therefore, the best way to discover which system a person uses is to listen patiently and observe. A visual person might be prone to taking notes and drawing, or just constantly looking at their surroundings. An auditory person might be quiet and attentive, whereas a kinesthetic person might be prone to talking with their hands. As you can see, there are many indicators of one's primary representational system, and I suggest you start practicing observing which system people use when you interact with them. Doing so will help you improve your communication abilities in general, as it will help you learn how to build rapport with others. Remember, communication is a two-step process.

The first step is to bridge the gap between you and the other person, which can be done by matching body language and voice. This will greatly help you get in sync with the other individual. The second step is to get the message across. There are several simple methods you can employ in your daily life to accomplish this.

Communication entails a lot more than just the spoken word. It consists of roughly 55 percent body language, 38 percent posture (including gesture and eye contact), and only 7 percent verbal content. NLP analyzes and utilizes this information to provide you with effective communication techniques. One easy exercise to do at home: get a pen and hold it horizontally in your teeth for a few minutes. Holding a pen in your teeth forces you to make a facial expression that is indistinguishable from a smile, essentially forcing you to express happiness. It may seem silly at first, but it will bring awareness of how you can improve your emotional state and confidence, even if it means holding a pen in your mouth before going out to your next meeting. The idea that activating a certain facial expression will automatically activate the emotion associated with it is called the *facial feedback hypothesis*. There is plenty of interesting research detailing its effect on our mood and how it can influence our everyday life.

Another key technique in NLP is referred to as *content reframing*. Let's say that your job comes to an untimely end, possibly because of an incident at work or due to circumstances outside of your control. While this may seem objectively negative on the surface, it is possible to reframe the situation in a positive light. For example, what are the benefits of being unemployed? Although this sounds discouraging, you're now open to other potential job opportunities. You now have the freedom to do what you want, when you want. And hopefully, you've learned valuable lessons from this job that will open up even better future opportunities.

Business Key Code

Old systems and paradigms have to break down before they can be replaced. Breakdown is the precursor of breakthrough.

Let's dive deeper into talking about the second keyword in NLP, *linguistic*. Comprehending the importance of working on the way we communicate with ourselves is a slightly more complicated matter. First, let's become aware that we filter the world around us not only through our physical senses but also through our beliefs, principles, and values. These are abstract concepts that we all hold dear to our hearts, created within us simply by experiencing life events, by modeling after other people, and carrying out simple interactions in our daily life.

Scientists believe that once we reach age thirteen, our beliefs and values are strongly developed in our brains and shape the way we see the world. This means that not only do we narrow down our reality to 126 bits of information, but we also interpret and therefore distort those 126 bits according to our personal views. Once these two "filtering" processes have happened, we finally make a picture in our heads to comprehend our recent experience. These internal representations you make are not just visuals; they are often enriched with sounds, smells, feelings, and even symbolic messages or meanings you have attached to them. These representations can often be more damaging than helpful. When you create a negative internal representation of an experience with negative self-talk, you inevitably change your mood to a negative one. Your body language, intentions, and energy are all affected. This slippery slope of negativity inevitably hinders your ability to reach your goal. By choosing to create positive internal representations about what you experience each day, you completely change how you experience the world. You will have the power to choose to live and a positive emotional state, which is the best state to be in when chasing your goals.

Before ending this chapter on NLP, I'd like to draw your attention to one more important concept. Introduced by Robert Dilts, it will improve your perspective on where to initiate change in your life. Dilts vividly described a person's inner being as a series of layers, each deeper than the last and each representing a different part of an individual's personality. The primary and deepest layer is the spiritual layer, followed respectively by identity, belief, capability, behavior, and environment. Dilts believes that for change to be the most impactful and long-lasting, it must happen at the deeper levels (*spiritual* or *identity*). The logic behind this is that a change at a deeper level will seep into the more superficial layers and affect the entirety of your being.

This principle also applies when we make negative generalizations about who we are. For example, let's say your boss asks you to put together a last-minute presentation that needs to be ready by the next day. You cannot complete the entire presentation, and your boss becomes angry with you. As we've learned in this chapter, you are the one who decides how to react to this event. You might put this at the environmental level and say something like, "I could not concentrate at work because there was too much noise around me." You could put it at the behavioral level and say, "I was not prepared to put this particular presentation together." You could even question your own capability and say, "I am not good enough at making presentations to put this one together." Finally, you could take it to an even deeper level and say something like, "I believe I do not fit in at this job" or "I believe I am not good enough to work here." As you can see, all it takes is combining a single mistake with a negative thought pattern, and suddenly, you have created a belief inside yourself that limits your ability to flourish and achieve your goals.

As you may have guessed, NLP has become popular recently because of how well it describes processes we all have in our heads but remain oblivious to. All these processes affect our everyday life and our ability to reach our goals.

The last letter in NLP, *programming*, can simply be described as the act of employing neurolinguistic techniques as tools to achieve one's goals. This business handbook's intention is to provide you with a vast arsenal of resources to change your life for the better. NLP is just one tool you can use. This journey will prompt you to transform at the deepest internal level, the spiritual one, where change is most complicated but can yield the most incredible results.

DAILY EMPOWERMENT AFFIRMATION

It is okay for me to have exactly what I desire.

THE WRAP-UP: ALL YOU NEED TO KNOW

✹ Discipline turns desire into reality.
✹ The first letter in NLP (*neuro*) refers to our five senses. These senses let us interact with our environment.

❀ The second letter in NLP (*linguistic*) describes the process of communicating ideas, to ourselves and to others.

❀ The last letter in NLP (*programming*), describes how we use neurolinguistic techniques to give our minds new ways to achieve our goals.

❀ Life is full of cause and effect, and NLP helps us to differentiate between a lifestyle of cause from one of effect. Living your life "at cause" is how you can embrace your mistakes and create future success.

❀ Be aware of your past patterns and behaviors. There is no failure, only feedback.

❀ With the right goal in mind, the right thoughts and beliefs, and consistent positive actions, you will reach your destination.

CHAPTER

3

❈

RAISING THE QUALITY OF YOUR MIND

To prepare yourself for the journey of change, you must have *accountability*. It is not an easy thing to hold yourself accountable, as doing so requires complete honest with yourself. However, few things in this world are both easy and worth doing. Accountability is merely one milestone we must push ourselves toward to achieve greatness and peace of mind. When we think of accountability, our mind often wanders to the concept of debt and attaches negative connotations. We are held "accountable" for our bills, our production level, and for the hours in a day we commit to our job. Now is the time to stop thinking of accountability in terms of being held responsible by others and to start thinking in terms of taking ownership of your life and holding yourself to a certain standard. From now on, when you think of accountability, think of your willingness to be fully responsible for your actions. Think of a commitment to generating positive results for the sake of your own happiness, success, and honor.

If you're the CEO of a company, obviously, you're responsible for the fate of your company and the well-being of your employees. However, rarely does a CEO truly consider the deeper, wide-reaching implications of their accountability. Does their company have a negative impact on the world around them? Does the general populace benefit from their existence? Is the environment damaged by the company's actions? A CEO is obligated only to do what is legally necessary, but an accountable CEO is a leader figure who takes selfless action to ensure their impact on the larger world is a positive one. Whether you're the CEO of the company or the lowest employee on the totem pole, you are accountable for the consequences of your actions. Although accountability may sound like a burden, a society full of accountable individuals benefits everyone. When everyone knows what must be done and what roles must be taken on, work is completed more efficiently than ever. Without accountability, roles become confusing and vague, and employees waste time rather than use it well. Unfortunately, this lack of accountability has become the norm and can be seen manifesting in most modern organizations. It seems as if someone is always willing to slap their face on a winning brand and take credit for all the good press, but the moment a serious challenge or lawsuit arises, you cannot find a single soul willing to be the face of the company. A leader should be fearless and cunning in the face of adversity, but instead, many of today's "leaders" are accountable for nothing and stick around only for the good times. Only by embracing total accountability can we begin to make a difference in our own lives and in the world around us.

BUSINESS KEY CODE

When you live your life within your values, you experience true fulfillment.

THE CONSCIOUS AND SUBCONSCIOUS MINDS

The most significant change you can create is a change in your consciousness and behavior to better express your authentic nature. This type of change brings us the best possible results. We are fortunate that we can change our thoughts, attitudes, desires, behaviors, associations, and environments. We are either the agents for positive change or the victims of change—the choice is yours. Your mind contains two distinct components with two discrete functions. These are the objective and subjective minds, the conscious and the subconscious minds, the waking and sleeping minds.

Picture these two minds performing two separate functions. Everything you think, speak, hear, and observe is going into your subconscious mind all day long. So be very careful what you are releasing and absorbing from these outlets. You must think and speak thoughts of peace, success, happiness, and love. This starts a chain reaction of cause and effect. Everything you do in the subconscious realm is replicated—as if by photocopier—into the physical, tangible world. Every thought is a cause, and every change to the world around you is an effect. For instance, when you are in a state of fear, your subconscious mind receives and releases a signal of terror, causing you to attract fearful situations.

The mind is complex and is capable of processing thoughts and emotions on myriad levels. Emotions have a strong impact on our minds, and conversely, emotions are also powerfully influenced by our mind's thought processes. There is a conscious and a subconscious aspect to your mind, a rational and an irrational mind. The thoughts and fears from your conscious mind drip down and stagnate in your subconscious mind, which in turn, introduces irrationality and hesitation into your actions, using your conscious mind. The subconscious mind is a throne that waits for your positive or negative emotions to settle in and rule over everything.

Good thoughts manifest good results, and negative thoughts manifest outcomes we wish to avoid. The subconscious mind is a sponge for new ideas and a powerful tool for creating a new reality. The quality of your life and your experience depends on the quality of your thoughts, your awareness of what's available to you, and your visions using your subconscious and conscious minds. There is untold power within you that can bring your life more happiness, joy, love, and success. You need not search for this power; you already possess it. Within your subconscious mind lies all the wisdom, knowledge, and understanding you could ever need. Within your mind, you can explore and discover a solution for every difficult situation.

Our adventure into this new consciousness begins by approaching each experience as if it is brand new. Greet each situation and person as if meeting them for the first time. If we branch out with no fear and live with authentic positive energy, we will experience various new incredible results. Kindness, love, joy, wisdom, happiness, and patience are qualities that never get old. You will come up short of your full potential until you learn how to love yourself and others unconditionally, have compassion for everything and everyone in life, let go of your old beliefs, quiet your mind, and trust yourself.

What we take into our body and minds has a profound effect on our vibrations and our health. Think of vibrations as a mind-body-spirit connection, or the rate at which our nervous systems and cellular structure harmonize with the frequencies of the universe. A sluggish vibration results from bad eating habits, bad energy, stress, and negative thoughts. By contrast, a powerful vibration results from well-rounded habits that keep us active, positive, and healthy. The power of your mind is always at work, but you must be ready and willing to receive strength and wisdom from it. Your every action and thought is *now* always aligned with your intentions.

READY, SET, TAKE ACTION

Brilliant scientists, writers, and inventors understand the power of the conscious and subconscious minds. Using their teachings, you can unleash your potential by harnessing the power of the two minds. To release old, negative patterns and habits, you must take four simple steps:

1. Release and forgive old thoughts or memories that would stop all the positive energy from entering your life.
2. Heal your emotional wounds with love for yourself and others.
3. Uplift your mind to a higher frequency of consciousness by expressing heartfelt gratitude and confidence.
4. Take time out of your busy business schedule and allow your conscious and subconscious mind to speak to you. It speaks to you through intuition, which manifests itself as a wish or desire. When we learn to trust this intuition, we rarely make mistakes because we are guided by the wisdom of our inner voice.

AFFIRMATIONS

Affirmations can retrain the subconscious mind to believe what you think and what you tell yourself. Affirmations propel you into a positive mindset. People who are positive tend to be more motivated, and when you are more motivated, you take action in your life and work harder to attain your goals. To see the truth in this, just think about the state you are in when you are depressed. It is usually hard to get motivated. You don't want to get out of bed, you don't want to go to work, and every task seems like a huge chore. On the contrary, when you are in a happy, positive state, you bounce out of bed, excited about what the day will bring.

Affirmations are a good way to keep you positive and thus motivated. For example, "Today, I am strong, competent, and confident in all areas of my life." Even if you don't feel this way right now, saying this affirmation multiple times a day will help you start believing it through repetition alone. Reciting affirmations will also retrain your brain to think more positively in general. It is so easy for humans to think negatively, to worry, and to expect the worst. Retraining the brain to think positively can help change your thoughts from doom and gloom to hope and joy. What you believe directly influences how you act, so changing your thoughts is vital when seeking to change your actions.

BUSINESS KEY CODE

Commit to confidence in yourself, your service, your business, your relationships, and everything that is a part of your career.

RECALL AND ACTIVATION

Believe it or not, there is something all human beings on earth have in common. We have good days and we have bad days. For those of you still wondering, the unfortunate truth is that no matter who we are, none of us can completely avoid the bad days. Everyone, from the lowest employee on the totem pole to the CEO of the company to the leader of the country, is subject to this curse. With this knowledge in mind, the next question is, "What can I do about it?" Luckily, humanity has been around long enough to have devised a few concise answers to this dilemma. Although negative events and the emotions they stir up may be unavoidable, we can always focus on regaining control over our feelings in the moments to come. The key is to make sure that when you recognize you have entered a state of negativity, you immediately take action to improve your mentality.

Drawing upon the energy of a fond memory is a deceptively simple but shockingly effective technique. Visualization is a concept we will discuss in depth later, but for now, let's discuss its most basic principles.

It's not powerful enough simply to imagine something. You must also vividly picture your emotional state in that moment and how your physical senses respond to your surroundings. In this case, rather than using visualization to manifest your goals, you will use it to reincarnate a previous emotional state and instill it within our present consciousness. Begin by recalling a pivotal moment in your life, something you will hold dear to your heart as long as you live. Maybe it's the day you finally received your promotion, the day your career really took off, or something from your childhood. Now, find yourself a quiet, comfortable place, and begin to reminisce about this life event. Go within yourself as much as possible, even to the point where you start to lose touch with your present reality. Fill your mind with details and sensations from that moment. Don't just recall a feeling of happiness. Try to remember how your happiness was so powerful, you felt there were butterflies rising in your chest and you couldn't keep that big smile from creeping across your face. Try to remember how it felt when you couldn't help but clasp your hands together in excitement or how the sides of your mouth grew sore from smiling so much. Involve whatever details bring your unique memory closer to your present reality. Was there a smell in the air or a sound from another room? Perhaps you just saw something so beautiful that your eyes widened and you couldn't turn them away for even a second.

Even if your memory is just a fantastic meal in Italy, try to remember the mouthwatering taste of the food. Lose yourself in this moment, and you will immediately elevate your emotional state. End this process by slowly returning to your present reality, all the while keeping the vivid, pleasant memories at the forefront of your mind. You should now notice a beneficial change in everything, from your body language to your thought processes. To be clear, you should never repress or try to forget your negative emotions. They are valid feelings that will always remain a part of you. However, once you've felt and processed the emotion, there is no reason to keep it lingering around—particularly if it's not pushing you toward success. No matter what your situation is, allowing yourself to stew in negativity will always be objectively unhelpful. The point of this exercise is not to make you forget your troubles but rather to help you remember the source of your strength.

CLUTTER

Too many material possessions, or simply an inability to throw things away, can lead to excessive clutter. A cluttered environment can be a strong indication of a cluttered mind. In the timeless practice of Feng Shui, it is taught that clutter creates energy blocks in all areas of life, including relationships, finance, career, and family. Take a moment to look around your environment. Carefully observe your home, car, and office, and see what areas could use a good decluttering. Perhaps a charitable donation of old items is in order. Taking action now and seeing the results of a clean environment can create motivation and open up space for all types of opportunities to attract and receive what you desire.

THE FLOW OF ENERGY

Every second of every day, we are putting our focus on something and therefore putting our energy toward it. When we wake up, we are putting our energy toward finding the courage to roll out of bed. In the middle of the day, we are putting our energy toward reflection and strategizing. And even at the very end of the day, we are putting our energy toward getting some sleep.

That's a simplistic of the process, but in reality, we often devote more of our time to negative thoughts and habits than to positive ones. When we dwell on our fears and doubts about the past or the future, we limit the total time during the day we could have spent on necessary and helpful thoughts and actions. No one on this earth can idly, effortlessly, or thoughtlessly lament on their past or dread their future. It takes a toll on our free time and our spirit to dwell on negativity, and we must remember this whenever we feel ourselves starting to fixate on situations that lower our emotional state. Focus on taking the energy you devote to negativity, and immediately put it toward positive manifestation. Although riches and perfect happiness may not fall from the sky the instant, if you redirect your energy flow, I can assure you that at least your mood will lift, your motivation will return, and your resolve will strengthen.

If having full control over your energy were a mindless task, it wouldn't take the time and practice it does. When you strive for mastery over your mind and energy, you'll at least be confident you're putting your focus toward positive actions and correlating thoughts with the clear intention of self-improvement. Let's go over a few easy techniques you can use anytime negativity creeps back into your mind and spirit.

First, get down to the bottom of what exactly is bothering you. Often, we get so caught up in the emotions of the moment that we feel compelled to act in ways that don't behoove us and seem strange to us later on. So, before you dwell on the negative to the point of developing depressing thought patterns and springing into self-destructive action, take a moment to identify what's bothering you, and redirect energy to solutions instead of diving deeper into hair-pulling and nail-biting.

Think back to when you began to feel this way. Then think of a time when you never felt this way before. Combine these two epochs and viewpoints to form a better understanding of how you developed these negative emotions in that span of time. If you have a clear recollection of what triggered such a fearful state, you will know more about the root of the issue and have a clear memory of exactly how you felt just before you accessed this negativity. Doing this will give you a boost toward a positive headspace and allow you to focus on what you're doing right now, in the immediate moment, to improve yourself or your life. Make sure you devote absolutely 100 percent of your energy and attention to accomplishing whatever will take you to the next level. You can do this anytime you feel yourself getting washed over by a wave of negativity simply by recalling, identifying, and refocusing your state of being.

Now let's touch on using the *power of intention*, which we will dive into later in this handbook. Go deep within your mind and soul and recognize which treasured desires you hold closest to your heart. Be clear about what you do want, but also be clear about what you don't want. Devote time each day to getting excited about the future, reaffirming to yourself that your future will entail all the incredible things toward which you have decided to devote your energy. To feel better and achieve more, replace pessimism and despair with passion and drive about what you're doing at this very moment. Don't ever let yourself get impatient and hopeless. Instead, become motivated and excited. Make a mental note and a resolution to yourself that every time you feel any distress or recurring thoughts of depression, you will immediately redirect your attention and energy toward planning or bringing about something spectacular.

This is the time to embrace an action item, such as running, biking, swimming, dancing, or any exercise that increases your heart rate. The act of exercising will release feel-good endorphins into your body and brain and help you to reset and reactivate a positive flow of energy. Staying consistent with action items leads to long-term changes, which lead to greater mental and physical health and a better overall quality of life. You don't have to be an Olympic athlete or professional bodybuilder to get these amazing benefits from exercise. You simply have to be willing to take action and put in the time. Don't waste effort on unpleasant thoughts and bad habits that drag down your emotional state. There's nothing stopping you from thinking positively and making your next action something that contributes to your future. Taking a moment every day to reflect on your emotional state of mind will help you stay grounded and step into your authentic self.

BUSINESS KEY CODE

When you choose to go with the flow of change, you have the opportunity to experience a sense of inner peace and personal empowerment.

THE POWER OF CHOICE— THE STAIRWAY TO SUCCESS

You have the power of choice, and we must remember that we all have the power and freedom to create new thoughts and actions. When you choose to experience yourself as successful and happy, you activate your power of choice regardless of circumstances in your life. The residue of yesterday's thoughts, beliefs, ideas, and actions is still clinging to you. You must let all this negativity go and live 100 percent in the *now*.

Being in the new reality, the future arrives through our emotions, visions, and creative ideas. Our thoughts and dreams are brought about by our actions in the present. Do not judge yourself by appearances. You are not the material world. You are an individual and a powerful being. You must give yourself the permission to love yourself, trust yourself, and consider yourself to be *enough*. Energy moves through your mind and emotions, then out into the manifested world that we call reality. When we open and expand into the transcendental realm, we are open to receiving higher thoughts, and our minds are filled with thoughts of love, happiness, joy, and prosperity.

Begin to contemplate what you believe and who you are. Feel connected to an eternal pure frequency and energy. By sending thoughts of love daily to your consciousness, you realize that the power of choice means you can finally focus on whatever you want to focus on and become. You will be in a position of power because your conscious mind will make choices that honor your higher self, a version of you that is always successful and happy and acts in line with the core of your true authentic self.

No matter what happened yesterday, you can begin your life again at this very moment. Remember, you are not the sum of the material items in your life. You are a force of free energy, and therefore, you are intelligent, talented, and capable of choosing a high-quality life and a business that feeds your passion. Today, you're creating a new character, a new script, and a new title for your movie. There is always more wisdom in the universe for you to access during your transition from confusion and despair to clarity and authenticity.

DAILY EMPOWERMENT AFFIRMATION

I am fully awake and living my vision.

THE WRAP-UP:
ALL YOU NEED TO KNOW

- ❀ Holding yourself accountable is difficult because it requires being completely honest with yourself.
- ❀ Staying positive manifests positive results, and being stuck in negativity brings more negativity into your life.

❀ Accountability is a willingness to be fully responsible for your actions and thoughts.

❀ Your subconscious mind contains all the wisdom, knowledge, and understanding you will need on your journey to success.

❀ When you break all limitations you set for yourself, you can achieve goals outside what you thought possible.

❀ Well-rounded habits keep us in alignment by making us stay active, positive, and healthy.

❀ Set a deadline or date for your goals. Do it. No matter what happened yesterday, you can begin your life again at this very moment.

❀ When things are destined to be yours, they come to you effortlessly. When things are not, there is nothing you can do but trust the process and relinquish control.

4

EMPOWERMENT AT YOUR DISPOSAL

In life, we are often our own worst enemies. We bombard ourselves with negative self-talk, believing we can "never" accomplish anything. We compare ourselves to others and beat ourselves up for our mistakes. These are just a few examples of how we do ourselves more harm than good. Typically, we are hardest on ourselves before we are critical toward others. Why are we so quick to judge ourselves harshly, to look at ourselves in such a negative light? Sometimes the issue stems from our upbringing. If our parents were harsh, critical, or judgmental toward us, we will be accustomed to this mindset. Repeating and then believing all our negative thought patterns and self-doubts becomes a habit. We think small, believing we aren't good enough for a promotion, a better career, or our material desires. This destructive self-talk, stemming from our fears and insecurities, leads to regrettable actions that don't support our highest self.

In psychology, there is a very interesting and well-established phenomenon called the *self-fulfilling prophecy*. According to this concept, an expectation an individual holds about a future event will inevitably influence that future event and cause the outcome to align with the expectation. We observe examples of this everywhere in our lives. For example, you wake up, and the first thing you tell yourself is, "Business was terrible last month, and it's not getting any better." This negative mindset will influence your behavior for the worse, causing your external circumstances to worsen. Let's say that you are about to close an important sale, one in which you have invested hard work and preparation. However, regardless of your business prowess, you are still not emotionally stable and feel anxious about it. This anxious state makes you tell yourself, "I will fail," or worse, "I am not skilled enough to succeed."

Perhaps you are already a big success in your field, holding a position many others envy. But with more success and power come more responsibility, and even a super-successful professional is just as susceptible to fear, depression, and self-doubt as any working-class individual. You could even be the president or CEO of a large corporation and begin every day by saying, "I'm going to sabotage this business and ruin it for myself and all the people under me." Once again, this negative mindset will influence your behavior, and more than likely, you will struggle to achieve success.

This concept has been proven in decades of research. Each of us can relate to it in our everyday life, and it can prevent us from expressing our full potential. So, let us be aware of when we fall into the trap of the self-fulfilling prophecy and strive to change our habitual thought patterns and create more positive self-talk.

By modifying our view of ourselves, we change how we feel about our capabilities, thus affecting the actions we take in life and thereby carving out the path to a brand-new life and a brand-new you! So, how do we go about doing this? First, decide what you want. However, you must think outside the box of your normal thought patterns that keep you small and prevent you from achieving the results you desire.

Start by thinking, "If I could have anything in life and money and time weren't issues, what would I wish for?" Write down the things you desire most. Start with your career. Are you happy with your career choice? Do you get up every day and look forward to your job and the day ahead? Do you like your boss and your coworkers? How do you feel at work each day? Do you always have to deal with a maelstrom of egos and drama? Do you go home at the end of the day exhausted, dreading the next day, when you must get up and do it all over again? Ask yourself what job or career would get you joyfully out of bed every morning, ready and eager to bring your whole self to the workplace. Perhaps you have a desire to start your own business, change your field of expertise, or fulfill a new passion. Write down all your career aspirations and just think to yourself, "The sky is the limit." Write down as many ideas as possible, as well as different ways to generate income. Some of your ideas may seem foolish to you now, but no matter what they are, writing them down will help you take the first step toward creating your dream life.

Next, think about your relationships. Are they fulfilling and supportive? Do they motivate you and fill you with life? Are they stagnant? Do they drag you down, draining you of your energy? Do you feel depleted after spending time with a person, or do you feel inspired and more energized? Write down all the relationships you have, including your friendships, romantic relationships, and family ties. Write down how you feel about them in terms of qualities you like or dislike and whether they bring you joy. Ask yourself if there are people you could oust from your life or who need more defined boundaries. Is it time to meet new people? Perhaps there is a meet-up you could join or a group aligned with your personal interests. The more people you meet, the more expansive your life can become. When your energy shifts to a higher frequency, you attract new people who share your mindset. The lingering energy and the individuals out of sync with the brand new *you* will dissolve away, and the clarity and awareness you need to build stronger relationships, self-trust, and inner confidence will flow to you effortlessly.

READY, SET, TAKE ACTION

These four exercises will help you find authenticity within yourself and identify and eliminate behavior patterns you no longer want. The goal is to remove any mental barriers or negative behavior preventing you from fulfilling your highest potential.

1. Make a list of the things that seem to recur in your life—the same interactions with people, the same results, the same job situations, whatever else repeats. Pay attention to negative thoughts, beliefs, attitudes, moods, and emotions that mimic those of your friends or family. Be aware of feelings of hopelessness, being lost, or victimhood.

2. Observe yourself during your interactions with others each day. Listen to the words you speak, take note of emerging emotions, and analyze the day's the events. Pay close attention to how you relate to people. It is crucial to remain authentic and compassionate toward all others. You will attract all you require; your life is your own creation.

3. Have a clear picture in your mind of the future, forgetting all obstacles, past or present. Then imagine yourself possessing and living your ideal situation. Keep a journal of how you feel when you are in the mindset of obtaining everything you desire.

4. Practice authenticity by embodying these qualities and traits as much as possible each day: intelligence, courage, spiritual knowledge, responsibility, consciousness, creativity, enthusiasm, forgiveness, happiness, and purpose.

BUSINESS KEY CODE

To transcend fear, you must be willing to risk. You must go beyond your comfort zone.

Write down everything you would like to manifest or receive. Perhaps this is a new home, a new car, or a fancy vacation. Maybe this takes the form of a spiritual awareness, healing, alignment, or awakening. Write down all the things you long for as if it were a shopping list. Use your creativity to generate new experiences that bring you happiness, solitude, and balance. Next, organize and narrow down your list.

Identify your priorities. What is most important to you? In terms of careers and interests, list the top three that bring you the most joy. When it comes to relationships, write down who is most important to you and who you want in your company. Clarify your goals. Perhaps this involves finding new friends, cutting out an old friend who drains your energy, or finding a new relationship. Maybe it requires strengthening a relationship that currently exists.

Whatever it is, make your intention clear to yourself and to the universe.

Now write down three activities that you know you can start the following month. Perhaps it is a class you have always wanted to take or a morning exercise routine you want to try. Whatever it is, make sure it's something that brings you joy, something that you would look forward to doing, something you won't end up quitting within a few weeks. Most people make grandiose resolutions to change, then never fully commit to a program or follow through. Make your goals attainable. Start slowly and take small steps toward establishing a new, positive routine, and before you know it, you'll be progressing by leaps and bounds.

Finally, go back over all your lists and choose three items you will prioritize. Write down not only the items themselves but also the action steps necessary to attain the specific results you're passionate about. Make sure your priority list aligns with the emotional state you want to achieve. Carefully consider whether your action steps will actually help you reach this state of mind. If it involves joining a class or seminar, you may want to write down, "Research different classes and seminars and find the one that suits me best." If you want to start a business, perhaps start by talking to others who have started similar businesses or watching interviews with people who are successful in that field.

Next, set a deadline for each objective on your list. If you'd like to attract a new work opportunity, write down when you want to have the new job and all the action steps you will need to take to achieve your timeline. If you wish to start a new business, generate publicity, or expand your network of clients, write down how soon you plan to accomplish these goals. Having deadlines lets the universe know you have put forward a strong intention and are willing to work hard to obtain your desires.

BUSINESS KEY CODE

Once again, remember that to bring your whole self to the workplace, you must remain in a state of calm, joy, self-love, and passion.

DO SOMETHING EVERY DAY

Look over your lists and choose one idea that inspires you to pursue your goals. Write down what end result you would like to achieve for the day and the steps you need to take. It is so easy to fall into habitual patterns and follow the same script every single day, only to realize years have passed us by and we are stuck in the same unhappy place as we were before. Perhaps it is the same job that does satisfies us or relationship that disappoints us but we remain in these situations because it is easier than stepping out of our comfort zone.

Some people seek comfort in the negative aspects of work they have become accustomed to, while others have a high tolerance for venturing into the unknown and conquering adversity. Find ways to take care of yourself as you expand your comfort zone. Discomfort can be a signal to avoid someone or something that will awaken a part of yourself that has been dormant. It's up to you to find and know the difference. We have to believe we can succeed at anything we put our minds to. This leads us to work at retraining our negative self-talk and taking positive action.

Also consider creating a business-mindset intention board. Intention boards are potent tools for visualization, and you can create one by putting words, pictures, and goals of what you desire onto a board, then hanging it in your office or your home and looking at it every day. The more an idea or goal resonates in your subconscious mind, the more your subconsciousness pushes you to work toward making it a reality. Just remember that anything is possible—if you can dream it, you can achieve it.

If you can get out of your own way, you can learn the necessary strategies to bring your dreams to fruition, then take the required action steps to achieve what you want to shape your reality however you desire. Life is short, so don't hesitate to work toward achieving your dreams, business and financial goals, and benchmarks of success.

DAILY EMPOWERMENT AFFIRMATION

I radiate success and shape my own destiny.

THE WRAP-UP: ALL YOU NEED TO KNOW

- ✤ Identify your values and make a list of what supports them and what hinders them.
- ✤ Deadlines let you put forth a strong intention and internalize your willingness to work hard to obtain your desires.
- ✤ Destructive self-talk, amplified by our fears and insecurities, causes our actions to fall out of alignment with our best selves.

❀ Simply be in the moment and say, "I know exactly what I want. I feel satisfied and complete."

❀ When it comes to business relationships, write down (or mentally note) who is the most important to you and who you want in your company.

❀ Check that you are not codependent. Set boundaries for personal responsibility.

❀ Be clear on what you do not want lingering in your life and the consequences of holding onto it.

❀ Admire and acknowledge what you desire, and it will increase.

CHAPTER

5

❋

ENTREPRENEURSHIP: HARDWIRED FOR SUCCESS

All top performers in their fields have something in common: they follow the typical routines and habits of people who are known for their success and their wealth. Almost all high achievers practice good time-management skills, exercise, eat healthy, and meditate. They use their time well because time is their greatest asset. They exercise and eat healthy because feeling good and nourishing their bodies is essential to their brain function and their overall abilities. Meditation clears the mind, relaxes the body, and allows new perspectives and ideas to emerge.

By combining these habits, millions have turned their lives around; however, others have unfortunately found that their weaknesses lie in their lack of positive habits. Even though people eventually become aware of their weaknesses, they often view these weaknesses as insurmountable and fear rising to the challenge. Others find new courage and strength within themselves, which allows them to overcome whatever is standing in their way, then create lives for themselves that allow them to enter the realm of success and abundance. This newfound courage and strength does not come from will-power alone but rather from perseverance. It's not important to succeed on your first try, but it is crucial never to give up.

One of the first important steps toward establishing positive habits and achieving success is to open yourself to new concepts, issues, and solutions. Soak up all the wisdom the world has to offer, and you will finally make serious progress in the right direction and become a leader in business.

Guard your finances closely, but don't be afraid to take risks. Opportunities need to be grasped before they slip away, but do not rush into anything you don't fully understand. Spread out your risk by investing your resources in ways that are proven and reliable, but diversify into newer, more exciting opportunities. In the last generation, we have witnessed drastic changes to all aspects of our lives thanks to revolutionary innovators like Elon Musk, Mark Zuckerberg, and Bill Gates. However, the next generation of entrepreneurs is still growing and honing their talents and will soon create unique and unfamiliar inventions that will push our societies farther down the path of progress.

Current trends should not detract from the ingenuity of future pioneers. An entrepreneur needs to know when to seize opportunity but also when to avoid new risks that harm their business. You can't make everyone happy, and you shouldn't put your focus on chasing everyone's acceptance. Instead, chase after dreams that guarantee your happiness. Cut out the excuses you make for yourself, discover the origins of your fears, and face your obstacles head-on.

If you don't know how to overcome a fear, begin by refusing to see yourself as a victim. Don't worry about what you don't have, and don't ever believe that life has placed you in doomed circumstances. Successful entrepreneurs confront their problems directly, which makes it easier for them to discover solutions and continue on their path to success.

MASTERING YOUR FUTURE WITH PERSEVERANCE

Some people are born wealthy, and others are blessed with natural talent in a certain field of work. However, this doesn't mean that all successful people are simply lucky or genetically gifted. Many simply persevere in the face of adversity, regardless of good or bad circumstances life has given them. All successful people start out with various different advantages and disadvantages, obstacles and opportunities. Remember this the next time you feel discouraged or overwhelmed, and you will quickly discover a powerful tenacity within.

This era of digital entrepreneurship is ever-changing, opening an entire new world of financial possibilities to anyone with an Internet connection. The work we do in offices, restaurants, and storefronts is being replaced with remote positions and automation at an unprecedented rate. Jobs that rely on a company or physical location have always been at risk during hard times, but in the modern era, it is even more precarious to carry such overhead. As it becomes more cost-effective for businesses to forgo hiring employees, they will instead purchase AI customer-service solutions. We will see the simpler, more common jobs fade out of the picture. Now more than ever, you have the chance to take hold of your future and pursue your inner entrepreneurial spirit. It all starts right now, with your intention to have a future without any financial dependency on another person or corporation.

In the pursuit of entrepreneurship, one of the biggest

challenges an individual may face is competing with large businesses who have built-in support teams for marketing, sales, and content, as well as access to endless funding. However, the silver lining is that an entrepreneur is able to join forces with these already successful companies in order to benefit themselves. This type of business alliance is not a form of financial dependency, but rather it is the utilization of the tools that are available in today's market. For example, one person may prefer to launch a product using a self-created website, while another person may wish to have their product listed on Amazon. One approach is not superior to the other because at the end of the day the success of the product will depend entirely on the strategies of the entrepreneur behind it. An entrepreneur of any age must always think creatively in order to launch a product or create a successful business. The key is to remain dedicated, enthusiastic, attentive, innovative, and always ready for any opportunity.

Everyone has to work hard to thrive and grow, but true freedom can't be attained by hard work alone. Each individual has an infinite amount of creative potential, and anyone who learns how to tap into that inner potential will quickly find themselves flying free of the burden of dependency on a steady job. This isn't to say people will ever stop working completely; however, like taking an early retirement, they will put all their efforts into their own success.

Working for a company and holding down a steady job is what people have done to survive and gain wealth for a long time. But in the end, the company always profits and benefits the most while the workers have to live off the scraps. This is a far superior alternative to avoiding work and earning nothing, but it is not the realization of the individual's true potential. We each need to look inside ourselves, find what drives us and what we dream of achieving, and then use that burning desire to create something that pays us back all the effort we put into it. Anyone who can do this will end up relying solely on themselves even in the most dire financial times simply because they learned how to use their own perseverance and creativity to provide security for themselves. Jobs may come and go, but anything you create and protect for your future will become your legacy and could even support your descendants and loved ones long after you are gone.

BUSINESS KEY CODE

Don't ask for permission to become an entrepreneur. Just get busy with your life and live your dreams.

ALIGN WITH PERSONAL EXCELLENCE AND COMMITMENT

The advent of technology in the business world has brought with it a number of challenges, but the variety of opportunities allows very different people to succeed in different ways. A person who is passionate about investing can access the stock market easier than ever before, thanks to the innovation of investment apps right on their phone. Someone who is more sales-minded can pursue product sales with ease thanks to the advent of online virtual stores and benefit from all the proceeds without ever having to worry about renting a physical storefront. Anyone who wishes to learn about starting a business has access to an infinite amount of invaluable information, instruction, and wisdom, passed down to them by others through the Internet. A person in the business world seeking career advancement can network online with other companies and executives more effectively than ever because of continuously advancing technology. The possibilities are endless, but you must find your passion and create your own opportunities.

Distinguish between goals and priorities. Goals allow you to focus on what you want to accomplish in the long term, but they often do not help you improve your habits and your lifestyle each day. Successful entrepreneurs focus their limited time and energy on what they deem to be most important, and they do this by setting priorities. A business leader who is unable to set priorities will often fall short of achieving their dreams simply because they will have too many obstacles to tackle at the same time or because their time and energy will be haphazardly dispersed. To set priorities that propel you forward, ask the following questions:

1. Do my priorities keep me focused on my goals?
2. Do I have a solid foundation of reliable priorities?
3. Do my priorities make clear what I need to do to achieve success?

If you can confidently answer these three questions, you should stay on your path and persevere. If these questions bring you uncertainty and anxiety, you need to take a step back, breathe, and reassess your priorities. If you have no doubt your priorities will lead you to your goals, you are probably correct, and you should focus on seeing your priorities through to completion. Take a little time every day to remember that you exist for a reason. Then move forward with purpose.

BUSINESS KEY CODE

A successful priority depends on a foundation of self-trust, self-love, and self-belief.

LEAD TO SUCCEED

Every company requires leaders at different levels of the hierarchy to properly function and succeed. Without strong leaders, employees of a company would face unnecessary confusion, stress, and instability. Leaders enable clear priorities and help keep all the different moving parts of a business organized. Similarly, an entrepreneur has to take on the role of a leader when they manage their own business. An entrepreneur might not have employees to lead, but they must apply the same leadership principles to their own business to succeed. Being a leader in life means being courageous and dedicated no matter what obstacles you face. In the same way a boss manages their employees to prevent unproductive or unprofitable actions, entrepreneurs have to manage themselves to make sure their own time is spent wisely. The greatest test an individual faces on the road to personal success is often the struggle to overcome their own weaknesses and to take action without being told to.

The business world has changed in more ways than just the technological advancements everyone has adapted to over time. For a while now, small businesses have been dying out while large corporations like Amazon, McDonald's, and Starbucks are acquiring more storefronts and more of the world's purchasing power. This seems daunting to many who dream of opening a business or trying to work independent from large corporations. The solution is to be a trailblazer in a field of business that you're passionate about and to see everything as an opportunity for growth and innovation.

READY, SET, TAKE ACTION

Take a closer look at the values that drive your desire to succeed. You need to identify these values, as they will strengthen your ability to lead others and succeed as an individual. You will gain clarity, make better decisions, and act with purpose. Write down everything you feel when you approach entrepreneurship, because how you feel will create situations that either discourage or motivate you. This will give you confidence about what you already have and what you need to do for your future. Put your focus on using your power of manifestation to create what you desire in the world of personal business.

1. List two core values that establish your foundation as an individual. Write down, in detail, what you hope for in the future of your business journey. Forget about the current circumstances, fears, and temporary challenges that are preventing you from achieving your ideal situation.

2. Write out habits that correspond to your core values. Write out any mental obstacles, attitudes, or feelings preventing you from being accountable for everything you do.

3. Change how you think about anything you consider negative about yourself. Fear of the unknown can be terrifying, but it results from your approach to fear. Change the way you think about fear, and let it bring

your attention to the areas of your life where you can avoid difficulty. Love and acknowledgment are essential when you want to understand yourself.

4. Train yourself for a moment to feel content and carefree for no reason at all. Feelings create the circumstances that have an energetic field that attracts a positive result. The next time you're expected to make an important decision or be a leader, use the core values and habits you wrote down as a guide.

CHANGE HAPPENS WHEN YOU STOP THINKING ABOUT IT AND ACTUALLY DO SOMETHING ABOUT IT

Everyone has a fear of failure, the same way everyone desires to succeed. The best opportunities often require you to take hold of them and will not simply fall into your lap. You never know how an opportunity will present itself, so keep an open mind and persevere without getting discouraged. Entrepreneurship brings unique benefits and opportunities, which is why so many people have pursued it and then found success. Opportunities have to remain special to us and somewhat hidden from us; otherwise, they would already be seized by others. Try to put away your past experiences when you make your future decisions. A person who is flexible in life and business is more likely to innovate and be considered a visionary.

Bringing discipline into your life means finally achieving the freedom you have always desired. When you focus your energy through desire and action, you create great results. Knowing your goals, your dreams for the future, and your desires will allow you to focus your endless supply of energy. Devoting all your time to entrepreneurship is easier said than done, and that is why so many people struggle on the path to financial freedom. Discipline and freedom are intertwined, and yet, people don't pursue discipline when they desire freedom. If you want more freedom in life or finances, cultivate discipline and positive habits. The internal or external obstacles you face now are simply helping you to gain wisdom so you can create a better future. Your whole life is in front of you, simply awaiting your command, your commitment, your persistence, your will, your energy, and your action.

DAILY EMPOWERMENT AFFIRMATION

"I am inspired to discover new visions for my life."

THE WRAP-UP:
ALL YOU NEED TO KNOW

✿ Any serious entrepreneurs face their problems head-on, which allows them to find solutions and strive for more success.

✿ Be responsible for creating every aspect of your life, and find the purpose and drive behind all your actions.

✿ Bring joy into your life. Take care of what you have, and don't worry about what you don't have.

✿ Individuals must be willing to overcome their own shortcomings if they desire to succeed. A person should take action because they feel compelled to, not because they were told to.

- ❁ Do what you're passionate about with excellence, and personal success will follow.
- ❁ Each individual has boundless potential for innovation, and anyone who harnesses their personal potential will quickly find they can depend solely on themselves.
- ❁ Remember to use your ability to manifest great results. It's easier than it sounds: desire it, obtain it, and accept it as yours.

CHAPTER
6

✦

THE MONEY MIND

S uccess with money is very much a result of your behaviors rather than your intelligence. Behavior is a subject even the very intelligent have great difficulty grasping. Someone very intelligent but lacking control over their actions or emotions can often end up in financial ruin. By contrast, the average person with zero education in finance can end up successful and in abundance if they possess a few key behavioral habits. Many people who are in search of money have lost sight of the importance of maintaining balance in their lives. All the money in the world will not make you happy if your life is an unbalanced disaster, so you must remember to seek happiness as well as wealth.

One of the most difficult skills in finance is the ability to stay positive and build good habits. Without a positive mindset and consistent action, we will constantly get in our own way because of greed and envy. A desire to be more successful than your peers can be healthy and motivating, but envy can drag you down to a lower frequency and inhibit your innovativeness. Happiness is results without expectations, so if your expectations are low and your actions are powerful, then you will generate more happiness. If you keep raising your expectations, then you may stay motivated but you will never truly be happy no matter how much you manage to achieve. You'll still feel just as unfulfilled as you did at your previous, less successful stages of life.

Many people do not believe there is a difference between wealthy and rich; however, this is not the case. Many errors have been made on the path to success because of a lack of knowledge in this key area. A "rich" person is someone who outwardly displays their prosperity, but "wealth" is an elusive concept. Someone driving the newest Ferrari is most certainly rich, but they are considered rich because they can afford to make the monthly payment on the car.

Wealth is quite the opposite: *wealth is what is saved and never spent.* It is much more important to be wealthy than to be rich, but so many people are only concerned about making their outward appearance a lavish representation of their economic situation. Many focus on schools, vacations, and houses, never stopping to consider investments or retirement accounts. When looking at a very rich person, you see their expensive car and property, but you likely don't see the expensive property they *didn't* purchase when they couldn't afford it. While you can always tell when a person is rich, but you cannot always tell when a person is wealthy, because their wealth sits inconspicuously in an asset or bank account. It is income that is never spent.

BUSINESS KEY CODE

Spending in excess to show others how rich you are is the fastest way to deplete your income. Wealth goes unseen.

People who consider money a safety net for their survival will never lose their wealth, but those who show off their riches at their own expense may soon find that they're falling out of balance with money. Society sees money as a key to happiness, and many people believe living and spending over their limits will make them more money or make them happy. The reality is that if you spend all of your time chasing money and none of your time seeking happiness, you may eventually find you never spent any time really living your life. Money is very powerful, but you yourself must be even more powerful. You must acknowledge yourself and find balance by forgoing greed and focusing on your personal journey. Wealth is delaying gratification and waiting until later, when the circumstances are more conducive, to buy that thing you want. Wealth is self-control, balance, and security. Don't be quick to judge others; focus on staying motivated and content with your own milestones of success.

READY, SET, TAKE ACTION

There are steps you can take to become more financially responsible and aligned with happiness. Write down all your anxieties, beliefs, and questions about money so you can begin to search for clarity. Put energy toward the power of money and possessing ownership over your thoughts about money. This exercise will let you examine your attachments to money and the value it brings to your life.

1. To elevate your economic situation and find balance, you must accurately assess your finances. You must tell yourself the truth about how much you have, not how much you can afford to spend right now. Write

out a full list of your significant assets, such as any savings, possessions, or investments.

2. Plan for how you will take care of any debts you might have. Stay in a positive mindset of abundance, but make a worst-case-scenario plan for how you will manage to stay on top of your debts under any circumstances. You detract from your future whenever you don't have a plan for right now. If your debts seem overwhelming, take confidence in starting immediately and maintaining consistency.

3. Put your ideal money situation into writing. Establish money milestones for three months, six months, one year, and five years. If you race past your milestones before their dates, rewrite your goals and give yourself a new challenge. Be the driving force of your financial success, not a victim of the situation you have created. Stay persistent and remember: you haven't failed until you've given up.

THE MYTH OF MONEY: BUYING HAPPINESS

Plenty of research is available online shows no correlation between becoming richer and becoming happier. Researchers often discover that wealthier people donate more impressive monetary amounts to charity, but proportionally they donate a smaller percentage of their income than people do in lower-income brackets. Many people, for either religious or personal reasons, believe in the rule that 10 percent of their income should be given away charitably, no matter how uncomfortable this makes their own life. By contrast, the top fifty wealthiest Americans, billionaires with seemingly infinite wealth, donate a tiny percentage of their wealth to charity every year. They may make significant donations, but they certainly do not adhere to a consistent rule for the sake of helping others. For example, Jeff Bezos was worth an unfathomable $160 billion in 2018, and he donated approximately $131 million to charity the same year. This number, $131 million, is awe-inspiring, which makes it easy to overlook that he only indeed donated 0.1 percent of his total fortune. It may seem insignificant when a person with $25,000 donates only a few thousand dollars. Still, in reality, it is a much more significant sacrifice than when a multi-billionaire donates hundreds of millions of dollars. Everyone can make a difference in their own way.

BUSINESS KEY CODE

We create our own conditions in life. Our attitude and approach determine the outcomes we receive. Happiness is not something that can be found or purchased; it is a state of well-being we put ourselves into. When we maintain a core belief that life is meant to be enjoyed, none of the setbacks and disappointments we face will distract us from our daily actions.

GENEROSITY AND ABUNDANCE

Researchers from Notre Dame examined the correlation between generosity and happiness at one point. They paid close attention to donations, volunteer work, and even relationships with friends and family. What they discovered was shocking; in general, people who gave away more of their money reported being happier than those who were less charitable and stayed in a scarcity mindset. There has been much theorizing that as wealth increases, generosity decreases. This may be because wealth can cause isolation, reducing happiness and charitableness. Often, inauthentic people try to manipulate or control successful individuals to further their interests. People making massive amounts of money, which can bring fame or celebrity status, are constantly worried about their relationships with the people around them. These highly successful individuals want to know if their acquaintances accept them for who they are on the inside or if it is all an act of status-seeking and manipulation. This situation causes the rich to distance themselves from people. The further isolated an individual becomes, the harder it is for them to find happiness. You can still achieve happiness as you see riches and success flow into your life, but beware the common pitfalls of isolation and negativity. Stay generous, because generosity will keep you involved in the community and in an abundance mindset. You must be open to receiving positivity and always looking for opportunities to be charitable with your money in a way that expresses gratitude.

You must accept what is rightfully yours while supporting others and accepting what is theirs to have. You have an important obligation to guide others to abundance and a responsibility to raise the frequency you embody when you are dealing with finances. It is up to you to establish how you will live your life regardless of your material wealth. When you leave this life, the only thing you will take with you is your emotional experiences, life lessons, and the joy and love you shared with your friends, family, and partners. The wealth you leave behind will be distributed to charity or family, but what is truly important is to enjoy each moment now that you are alive, healthy, and surrounded by loved ones.

There are endless opportunities for individuals to build confidence and gratitude in the business world. Much of this comes from being a productive person, which boosts self-esteem and appreciation for the opportunity. When one takes a positive approach to business, one grows one's character and sharpens one's abilities. A productive, confident person will generally be a happier, more successful person. Unfortunately, people often end up in roles that do not allow them to develop or improve. You must seek opportunities that will bring you a sense of balance rather than prioritizing money. Abundant living is staying aligned with your true path and appreciating anything the universe has envisioned for you.

DAILY EMPOWERMENT AFFIRMATION

The more money and resources I have, the more I can help others.

THE WRAP-UP: ALL YOU NEED TO KNOW

❦ People who treat wealth like a safety net for survival will always have enough, but those who spend beyond their limits for appearance's sake may quickly fall out of balance with money.

❦ Life is abundant. You can always have what you want.

✤ Life consists of love and effort channeled into commitment.

✤ Have a clear goal about the money you need now and will need in the future to live your dream.

✤ Don't put limits on your beliefs. Everything you need for your success is already within you.

✤ Catch yourself before your ego takes over your thoughts, words, and actions.

✤ There is no lack of solutions or possibilities.

✤ You can transform passion into profit.

✤ If you devote too much time to chasing wealth and none of your time to pursuing happiness, balance, and wellness, you may discover you never took the time to enjoy life to the fullest.

CHAPTER

7

❈

TAKING STOCK AND INVENTORY

If you genuinely wish to experience your authentic self and inner peace, you must learn to *let go* of your negative attachments. It is easy for the mind to dwell on past problems and mistakes. Let us remember these emotional experiences we recall disdainfully as nothing more than learning lessons. Begin to practice the power of forgiveness by letting go of the people or situations in your past that shamed you, hurt you, or made you angry. Forgiveness is the bridge between seeing yourself as unworthy and incomplete to seeing yourself as being centered and validated. Forgiving yourself helps you to feel self-love, self-respect, and self-validation. Forgive yourself and forgive the past, and then continue toward achieving your goals in business and life.

NEGATIVE ATTACHMENTS AND THE VICTIM MENTALITY

Negative attachments are thoughts echo in our heads. We expect the worst outcome to a business situation, and we can't stop obsessing over the situation we imagine. We think about how a conversation with someone will turn into an argument—or, worse yet, whether they will decide to stop doing business with us altogether. We think about an upcoming meeting at work or a conversation with our clients and how we might embarrass ourselves instead of imagining all the good that could come from it. Our minds tend to go to the worst possible scenario much faster than a positive one because it is wired to protect us from potential tragedies, such as bankruptcy or a significant loss of employees or accounts. And when we hope for the best but plan for the worst, we won't be devastated when the worst indeed occurs, since we are preparing and thinking about it ahead of time. Yet it would be far better to envision a positive outcome and strive toward making our hopes a reality rather than live in fear of failure or remorse.

We may get stuck in a toxic cycle of negative thoughts because of the victim mentality. We see ourselves as victims of the circumstances and don't believe we have any control over our lives or ourselves. When we are the victim in life, we say to others, "I was passed up for a promotion because my boss doesn't value me as a worthy employee" or "Things never go my way. I don't remember the last time anything went my way." The problem with the victim mentality is that it doesn't put us in control of our own lives. Instead, it leaves us a victim as though life is continuously beating us down. We must stop the victim mentality if we ever want to be successful, abundant, and joyful.

An excellent way to escape the victim mentality is to

remember that we are always in control of our lives. We are in the pilot's seat, creating our destination and every experience around us. Life is happening through us, not to us. Know that any goal you put your mind to, you can achieve. Any level of financial security you dream of, you can achieve.

BUSINESS KEY CODE

Persistence and trust are continued movements on a path to your objective.

FEELINGS OF FEAR, ANXIETY, AND INADEQUACY

Our fears and anxieties result from negative attachments, and if we want to create genuine happiness and peace, we must break free from these attachments. Often we become negatively attached to the approval we receive from others, not realizing the pitfalls of depending on others for recognition.

Wanting the approval of others is another way we develop the "victim mentality" in life. This victim mentality can be a cage that imprisons us emotionally. Seeking approval is putting our self-value and self-worth in the hands of another person. Sometimes we want the approval of others because we see them as being more valuable individuals than we are. This is just human nature, and each of us has a challenge we are on this earth to work through. We all face the major challenge of judging ourselves harshly, comparing ourselves to others, or never being quite good enough. No matter what is happening, maintain your confidence and self-worth, hold yourself in high regard, adjust your priorities, and continue toward your vision. Your title at work does not define you, nor does the embossing on your business card. You are energy with unlimited potential. No one is more or less valuable than you are. We are all unique and important, and when we recognize this fact, we stop relying on others to bolster our low self-esteem. You are a magnificent being with endless possibilities.

Sometimes we see individuals with a better job, or with a higher income, or in a more important role, and we think getting their approval will validate us, but this is a false hope. On a spiritual level, this individual could be just as unhappy and dissatisfied as we are, if not more. When we seek outside approval for ourselves, we willingly get onto a roller coaster ride of emotions. The individual we seek approval from may accept us one day but reject us the next. This leaves us feeling very unstable and off-balance. When we put our self-approval back where it should be, on ourselves, then we can feel much more peaceful, confident, and competent. We take our self-esteem back into our own hands and create more inner peace and stability.

The opposite side of this coin is a fear of the unknown and uncertainty about situations. We crave stability and assuredness in life because we feel out of control if we aren't exactly sure what the future holds for our business. When we feel out of alignment with ourselves, we try to control all other people and situations. Trying to control others means we don't have trust in ourselves or trust life can flow quickly and effortlessly without our having to manipulate everyone and everything around us.

Controlling others can lead to manipulation, domination,

lying, jealousy, and even bullying to get our way. What is underneath all this is insecurity. It means we don't have the trust in our authentic selves to direct our lives and find success in all areas. You can stand in your power and speak your genuine truth to anyone you interact with. If you can be authentic with family, friends, partners, bosses, or employees, you will never feel your inner self goes unheard and ignored. Now, let the authentic leader within you guide the way.

When we are life's team players, we become adaptable and flexible while retaining our authentic values. This teaches us to trust not only in the universe but also in ourselves. By working at building our self-esteem and our ability to make good decisions, we will have less of a desire to manipulate the world and all others around us.

READY, SET, TAKE ACTION

Another great daily exercise you can do at home or your workplace is what I call *taking a daily emotional selfie*. This is a daily exercise, and you can practice this to help prepare you for anything. Treat this as a daily rehearsal, the same way actors in a play memorize their lines until their subconsciousness has taken in all the words. As they do this over a while, and the words become an emotion; they toss the script of pages away. The emotional state of the energy takes shape, and then the actor's character becomes alive on stage or in front of a movie camera. This exercise is a simple four-step process.

1. Plan your vision of what you would like to create or manifest.
2. Hold on to this vision, and then pick up your cell phone as if you would take a selfie somewhere or with someone.

3. Take at least one minute to concentrate on the emotions created by achieving your result. Hold on to the excitement of that moment, and snap the photo. The emotional feeling is the key here.

4. Repeat this exercise daily for about twenty-one days, until the emotional state you visualized becomes real inside you. This will propel your projects, goals, and dreams toward profound success.

WASTEFUL SPENDING AND LIVING BEYOND YOUR MEANS

Many people become torn between the pressures of work and personal time, so they begin to overspend as a release or a justification for being overworked. Often even a successful, wealthy person lives far beyond their means. It is easy to inflate our sense of self-worth by purchasing material items. Still, very frequently, people go so far as to put themselves in debt to display a "Hollywood celebrity" image of themselves that is inauthentic. As the pace of life speeds up, the pressure to produce at your job or business increases, taking a toll on your emotions and performance. This often calls for significant changes in our lives, career, and relationships.

You need to get in touch with yourself to find the balance between work and personal life. You will create more business and attract more success by being authentic and functioning on a high emotional frequency. Your success in any business interaction is based on your ability to show your power, which stems from your thoughts and feelings about yourself. Potential clients and business partners will be driven away if your energy is negative, fearful, or insincere. You must always be prepared to learn as you are experiencing your life lessons; believe in yourself and dismiss any negative ideas, people, or influences that might hinder you from achieving your goals.

SO HOW DO WE BECOME MORE CONFIDENT?

You have undoubtedly heard the phrase "Fake it till you make it." It is often used in social psychology and in many other disciplines that study human behavior to summarize the idea that our mind and our body are very closely connected and that one can easily influence the other. By simply holding a pen in your mouth and thus forcing your facial muscles to smile, you will automatically become happier than you were before. There are a series of different things that you can do to move your subconscious and conscious mind into a better, more productive state, such as improving your frequency, body, and posture. For example, before a job interview or an important pitch meeting at work, stand in the bathroom with your arms raised to the sky, beaming a huge smile.

One of the core principles I have always taught is the *power of yes*. Exclaiming, "Yes! Yes! Yes!" excitedly into the mirror works on the same principle as the first technique of raising your arms in the air. It generates a positive frequency to manifest extraordinary results. This will help you go into any vital life or work event with more confidence and faith in yourself.

VISUALIZATIONS

Visualizations are another interesting way to become confident. If you can visualize yourself conquering the task at hand before an event, business meeting, speech, or an important

Skype or Zoom call, you will have a much higher chance of succeeding the way you visualized it.

NLP reveals it; psychology proclaims it. Everybody agrees that visualization is a powerful tool that works in tandem with affirmations to help you manifest what you desire in business or anything else in your life. One way to visualize is to find a quiet place where you will not be disturbed and close your eyes. Now bring up the event or situation you want to be confident in, and let that event play out in your mind's eye. Visualize it going well, and see yourself being that calm, centered, and confident person saying all the right things. Visualize the people around you responding positively toward you as well. Perhaps you will receive a promotion at work or an exciting new job offer. Whatever you must overcome, always visualize the positive outcome you desire.

BUSINESS KEY CODE

Visualize that amazing moment of accomplishment in detail, then commit that energy to the universe.

DO I LOVE MY JOB?

Life is short, so you should love what you do daily. Spending approximately forty hours per week at a job you hate going to, being miserable while you are there, and anticipating going home the entire time is no way to waste a good portion of your life.

What if you don't love your job? Make a list of the positives and negatives of your current line of work. See if the negatives outweigh the positives. If they do, then see if there is a different position within the company that you would like better and pursue that. Or perhaps it is time to think about an entirely different career field. Write down your career goals and where you would like to be in three months, one year, five years, and ten years. Write down what this entails—perhaps more education or some research on different career paths you would like to pursue. Get in touch with your passions and write them all down. What do you love to do outside work? So many people have turned their passions and hobbies into their work and got paid to do what they love!

Visualize your perfect career, your perfect job, and your perfect day from the time you get out of bed to the end of the day, when you lie back down for the night. Write down this perfect day. Then, look over your lists and see what excites you! If your current job isn't on there, then you have your answer.

WHAT IS YOUR BELIEF ABOUT YOURSELF?

What you believe about yourself becomes a reality. Write down what you believe about yourself, and then ask: Is this true? How do I know this is true? Do I want to change myself? If so, write down ten things about yourself that you would like to change. Turn these recognitions about negative attributes into positive actions, and write correlating affirmations that reflect your goals. Repeat them out loud as often as you like. Then incorporate the visualization aspect by picturing and accepting yourself as this new person.

HOW TO MANIFEST YOUR AUTHENTIC SELF

First, you might be asking what your authentic self actually is and how you know when you are living from it. One might say that being authentic is being genuine in your interactions with others, which takes vulnerability and the risk of being rejected. Getting in touch with your vulnerability is an excellent way to start living from your authentic self. Feeling more confident is also a result of living more authentically, because you will feel more assertive about your decision-making and your interactions with other people. You will no longer operate from behind a mask (also known as the ego). There is a stark contrast between an inflated ego and genuine self-confidence. Egotism is the phenomenon in which the mind believes you should be in control of everything because you consider yourself more intelligent and capable than others. In this headspace, we often focus on thoughts or ideas that reinforce our notion of self-importance. This outward appearance is off-putting to others, indicating insecurity rather than confidence. Only by accepting the situations we don't have control over and acting from a place of good intentions can we begin to exude authentic confidence for the world to see.

DAILY EMPOWERMENT AFFIRMATION

I welcome great change. Every day is full of opportunities for me.

THE WRAP-UP:
ALL YOU NEED TO KNOW

❀ Whatever you devote your energy and time to increases and grows because your energy and time cause opportunities to flourish.

❀ Visualize your perfect career, your perfect job, and your perfect day—from the time you get out of bed until you lay your head down for the night.

❀ Develop good behavioral patterns, and you will stop accepting that your situation is permanent.

❀ Visualize yourself overcoming the current obstacle you face, and you will have a more confident approach and a much higher chance of success.

❀ Always choose to be around the people who enhance your positive choices in life.

❀ You attract and repel conditions in your life according to your state of mind, beliefs, and thoughts.

❀ Your success in any business interaction is based on your ability to show your power, which stems from your thoughts and feelings about yourself.

CHAPTER

8

❖

BE YOUR OWN
WELLNESS GURU

We are all subject to stress and unfortunate happenings in our lives. Without question, stress will appear like a sudden thunderstorm. How we cope with this stress is the only aspect we truly have control over. Some people collapse when confronted with the slightest hardships, while others masterfully navigate the most devastating circumstances. Most of us function between these two extremes, but we need to learn to handle our "crises" in the most constructive and spiritually sound ways possible. If we can acknowledge the intense emotions of rage, guilt, and fear that surface during stressful and challenging times and not deny or suppress them, we will grow stronger and have a genuine breakthrough. Repressing these emotions does not make them disappear; on the contrary, all the negativity will find an outlet and manifest itself in another way, such as illness, brain fog, and fatigue.

Chronic or extreme stress may wear us down until we are husks of our former selves. Luckily, many techniques can help you control stress, but without awareness or regulation of your mental habits, the stress will quickly return and affect all areas of your life. Do not use the methods in this chapter solely for stress relief but also for altering those mental habits producing the recurring stress. For instance, meditation is a great stress-reducer that produces mental and physical changes and has been repeatedly validated in clinical trials by medical and psychological professionals. So how do we go about capturing and internalizing this new energy? How do we live life with a positive attitude amid overwhelming stress? So many of us neglect and abuse our minds and bodies because we are too tired, overworked, stressed out, and overburdened with responsibilities. Positive thinking, good eating, proper exercise, and meditation honor, preserve and respect the temple that is our body. These actions allow our highest level of spiritual energy to guide us through every moment of the day.

In this age of technological advancement, multitasking, and sixty-hour workweeks, the metaphor that equates our bodies with a sacred place reverberates with more meaning than ever. Destressing must be supported and accompanied by proper diet and regular exercise. Individuals must make better choices that support their inner intuition regarding what their body needs nutritionally and what does not serve them well anymore. This requires that you take full responsibility for your mental and physical health, recognizing what you cannot control, such as a busy schedule or bad habits formed in the past. You can start achieving results right now with three action steps: Conscious breathing, yoga, and meditation.

BUSINESS KEY CODE

Healthy people are not stuck emotionally. If you're physically and mentally healthy, nothing will obstruct your flow or the conditions of your life.

CONSCIOUS BREATHING

Proper breathing is an antidote to stress. We all breathe, but few of us practice the habit of deep breathing. When you inhale, you draw through your nose and down your nasal passageway. Your diaphragm stretches across your chest and separates your chest from your abdomen. When your diaphragm relaxes, your lungs contract and force the air out. This happens automatically and unconsciously, but you can also control your breathing to elevate your mood and clear your mind.

This is where correct breathing plays a significant part in providing your lungs with adequate fresh air to purify and oxygenate your blood. If the waste products in your blood are not removed and are kept in circulation, they will slowly poison your system. Your organs and tissues will become undernourished, and your digestion will be impaired. Lack of blood oxygen contributes to depression, irritability, anxiety, muscle tension and fatigue, and increased stress during difficult situations. Proper breathing habits are essential for your physical and mental health.

Conscious awareness of our breathing is a simple but

overlooked concept, and deep breathing is a wonderful tool for the mind and body. Before you start your day at work, you should take a moment to take several deep breaths to clear your mind and prepare for your day ahead. Breath is one of the most effective natural antidepressants available to us. It can refresh us like cool water on a hot summer day. So go ahead and take a deep breath, and then slowly release it. Do this three times to release tension from your body and become fully present. With each breath, follow it down to the opening of your lungs, then relax your diaphragm and allow your body to fill with air and expand. When you can't take in any more air, slowly begin to exhale and release the old energy. Take a moment to slow down and let your exhaling last twice as long as your inhalation. Feel yourself flushing out all the residual anxiety and stress through your breath.

You will experience immediate benefits from breathing deeply, but you must practice deep breathing daily to appreciate its full effects. For example, nervous people tend to draw short, shallow breaths into their upper chest. By taking long, slow, deep breaths, you should raise and lower your abdomen. Stopping your nervous breathing and mimicking a calm person's breathing will immediately help you feel calmer and more composed.

Try lying down twice a day and doing deep breathing exercises for ten minutes, increasing the time until you feel the tension leave your body. When you become proficient with breathing into your abdomen, practice breathing in this manner while you are sitting and standing. Concentrate on the movement of your abdomen—up and down—as you move the air in and out. Embrace the feeling of great relaxation that this will bring. Deep breathing exercises are being used today to treat and prevent shallow breathing, hyperventilation, and poor circulation in the hands and feet. Remember to breathe through your nose and practice good posture. Avoid tight clothing, as this interferes with circulation.

Breathing exercises have also been a cornerstone of yoga for many centuries. Yogis have used this discipline to control their bodies and minds and develop their mental, physical, and spiritual selves. Develop your own program of deep breathing or yoga exercises to release your daily tensions. You will stimulate your breathing, circulation, and nervous system. You will become more alert, gain new energy, release old tension, and cope with stress.

MIND-BODY VISION EXPANSION EXERCISE

Remember to spend time each day in tranquil and beautiful settings, to open and nourish your heart and mind. Make a conscious shift into a higher frequency by expelling old, negative energy and being open to new energy creating balance within you. Take ten minutes each day to imagine feeling no one can stop you from reaching your goals. You have unlimited potential, and you can expand your consciousness and vision to create your desired reality. Feel yourself uplifted into a higher existence of nonjudgment, where you allow all others and yourself to live authentically; remembering each of us creates what we desire for ourselves.

YOGA

Yoga is usually defined as "union" or "connection." This is a union between the limited self and the spiritual self. The original practice of yoga is an old discipline created in India. It is a metaphysical practice that uses breathing techniques,

exercises, and meditation. In Sanskrit, the word "yoga" sig-
nifies any form of connection. Yoga is both a state of connection and a body of techniques that allows us to connect
to anything. Yoga improves our quality of life and reduces
stress, anxiety, insomnia, depression, and back pain. It also
lowers heart rate and blood pressure. Many traditional yogic
paths facilitate connection to the highest truth and awaken
our consciousness, including tantra, mantra, laya, kundalini,
bhakti, jnana, and karma yoga. Each path specializes in its
own techniques and methods to awaken greater awareness
and connection to self and life. Several yoga practices include
posture (asana), breathing (pranayama), control of subtle
forces (mudra and bandha), cleansing of the body-mind (shat
karma), visualizations, and chanting of mantras, and many
forms of meditation.

So, how can you incorporate yoga into your life? The
key is that all yoga techniques help people become more in
tune with themselves and feel more connected. The secret of
yoga practice is awareness because yoga is another process
in the journey of self-discovery. With this in mind, you can
now turn to yoga when your life and business stressors are
overwhelming you. Although yoga is vastly perceived as a
practice meant to provide you with physical benefits, a keen
individual will also use it to improve their mental and spiritual
state. Don't do yoga only because your body needs a stretch;
do yoga because your spirit needs a boost.

MEDITATION

Meditation is an experiential exercise involving the use of
your focus and attention. It is not affected by your line of
work or thought processes but still helps you work toward
a psychological or physiological state of awareness. Records

on meditative practices date back thousands of years, it is something ancient and profound that has always been with the world and always will be.

Meditation is the art of listening to the spirit of the world and is also a form of healing. There are many forms of meditation, and any of them can be used to melt away the stress, fear, and doubt that's plaguing you. Many studies have shown consistent neurophysiologic patterns that occur during meditation. There is a slowing of one's breath and heart rate, decreasing oxygen consumption, and reducing your blood pressure and metabolic rate. According to some physiologists, this sudden reduction can be greater than it would be after six hours of sleep. Meditation can reduce your blood pressure and even stabilize it in some crises. The arterial concentration of lactate, a chemical sometimes correlated to anxiety, will drop four times faster in meditation than in simple rest. An electroencephalogram (EEG) will record brain wave changes or patterns during meditation that are different from those recorded during normal sleep. Since meditation is practiced while one is awake, the pattern it produces is characterized by inhibition of the sympathetic nervous system. This nervous system is responsible for our fight-or-flight response. In other words, it creates a state of relaxation which is even free from your body's most primal feelings of stress.

The practice of meditation seems to alleviate stress-related disorders and prevent the adverse effects of typical daily stress. To practice meditation, you must learn to sit quietly and close your eyes for two periods of twenty minutes each day. During this time, you vacate your mind (the stress battlefield) and elevate yourself into a state of "restful alertness." You can reach this state by concentrating on the silent repetition of a word, which is nothing more than a meaningless sound. As a result, your hands and feet will probably feel heavy and tingle, and your mind will be vacant of chattering thoughts.

If used properly, meditation can enhance your life by helping you maintain and increase your health and activity. You can also try using meditation at work during your lunch hour or before a meeting. Some people even experience better sleeping habits after meditating for a while because stress is the natural enemy of sleep. Stress keeps you awake and deprives your body of the relaxation it needs as a relief from the tensions encountered during the day. Meditation seems to initiate better overall health habits through changes in lifestyle, which plays a big part in improving reactivity to stress. When you can reduce stress, the results will show up clearly in your energy level, coping capability, creativity, business mindfulness, and overall personal health.

Initially, meditation will be felt physically, as your musculature will relax and release tension. But there is also an attitudinal component to meditation which is equally important. Opening the hearts and minds through meditation has become a new standard of mindfulness at work for top companies like Microsoft and Google. By improving and developing the quality of your inner self, you improve the quality of your communication and relationships at work. You alone are responsible for ensuring that meditation enhances your life. It is something you do by yourself, for yourself, to know yourself better.

BUSINESS KEY CODE

The quiet and the space of stillness are where we must move to be abundant, tranquil, and supported.

RELAXATION TECHNIQUES

Most of us do not realize which muscles are chronically tense in our bodies. Progressive relaxation can help you identify which muscle groups tend to be tense. It will help you evolve from tension to deep muscle relaxation. You may practice this technique lying down or sitting up in a chair. Learn to tense each muscle or group of muscles from five to seven seconds, and then relax them for twenty to thirty seconds. Depending on how tense your muscle is, you may repeat this process up to five times. Repeat this procedure for other muscle groups until you feel the relaxation develop. You must remember to use moderation when tensing some of your muscles in the neck or back to avoid muscle or spinal damage. Excessive tightening of your toes and feet may also cause cramping. Once the technique is familiar to you, focus your attention on just one muscle group at a time. For example, a major muscle group that is commonly tense is found in the hand, forearm, and bicep.

Now relax in a comfortable position and clench your right fist. Tighten it, and then study your fist, hand, and forearm tension. Now relax and feel the contrast between tension and looseness. Repeat the procedure with your left fist several times, and finally, tense and relax both fists together. By bending your elbows and tensing your biceps, you will feel a tautness in your upper arm. With enough practice, this technique will help you attain the desired effect of total body relaxation in just a few minutes. Initially, you will want to spend at least twenty minutes tensing and relaxing to release tension from all your muscles and their fibers.

This relaxation technique could easily be considered a form of meditation, but it is simply another simple tool for stress-release you can always carry. When you employ conscious breathing, yoga, meditation, or any other method of releasing tension, you are taking the important first steps toward feeling better. If you can't relax and align with your authentic self when you're alone and peaceful, you can't expect to bring your whole self to the workplace or any other important aspect of your life. Stress is just another bump in the road to mind-body-work balance, and I hope by now, you're feeling more knowledgeable and prepared for life and work than ever before.

DAILY EMPOWERMENT AFFIRMATION

I release all stress from my mind and body. I remind myself that life supports me and wants me to be happy.

THE WRAP-UP: ALL YOU NEED TO KNOW

- ❀ Each experience in your life is an opportunity to move you deeper into your spiritual quest.
- ❀ Be aware of your body, reactions, thoughts, and feelings from moment to moment.
- ❀ By taking responsibility for your mental and physical health, you are waking up your awareness.
- ❀ Although yoga is often thought of as a way to exercise for physical benefits, many enlightened individuals also use it to enhance their mental and spiritual state.
- ❀ Meditation can maintain and enhance your health and activeness even if practices only a few moments.

❀ Slow down by cutting things out, and really simplify your life.

❀ Look at why your life is as busy as it is, and ask yourself, "What are the consequences of this?"

❀ As you change your busy schedule and get rid of bad habits formed in the past, you will begin creating new opportunities for relationships in business and the quality of your relationship with yourself.

CHAPTER

9

✲

THERE'S NOTHING
HOLDING YOU BACK

How can we create a winning attitude at work? How do we build strong, healthy relationships? How do we embrace a growth mindset, improve ourselves every day, and achieve everything we put our minds to?

Ask someone how work was, and you will usually hear complaining, groaning, frustration, or a "don't ask" comment. Most people aren't happy at work and will tell you all about why. Work is where we spend a significant portion of our time, and how we feel at work can spill over to how we feel in our personal lives and vice versa. Since we often spend most of our day working, we have to be extra cautious about how we feel at work and around our co-workers.

Once you've done something repeatedly, it becomes second nature, a comfortable habit. When you create large goals, you will have to adopt new beliefs and behaviors that contradict the old ones. The act of visualizing a new job or chain of events will help you to break old patterns. This involves evaluating your chosen career path and the direction you are heading in life. Whenever you plan the future, always ensure the present is tranquil. Make sure your plan always incorporates an element of joy, along with all plans you intend to fulfill. At this point, start trying to figure out what reignites your passion for life and pursue that. Sometimes, we need to pursue new and undeveloped business talents outside of our ordinary job to stay focused and positive in our current position. Putting time and energy into your intelligence and creativity may be more lucrative than trying to juggle multiple jobs.

If you decide you have already found your calling and, for the most part, you are happy, you need to look at ways to improve your experience while you're at work. One of the steps we can take is to improve relationships with our coworkers. If you build strong, healthy relationships with the people you spend a significant amount of time with, everything will flow easily and your production will increase. There can be many different types of personalities you are surrounded by at work, especially if a large company employs you. Some of these personalities can be extremely challenging to deal with. However, the key to success is to stop focusing on others and start focusing on yourself.

If you want your reality to change, then change your thought patterns and emotional frequencies. Begin by paying attention to your attitude. If you wake up and go to work with a negative mindset, dreading the day ahead and all the people you will encounter, then doing your job and interacting with anyone will be an exhausting challenge. You can interpret other people's moods and emotions through their energy, so be wary of the energy that you emit. If your internal energy is toxic and you are putting that out into the world, you are guaranteed to get toxic energy back from the people who surround you. If this is the case, change your mindset to succeed in your workplace. If what you feel becomes real, you need to change your attitude about work and the people you encounter daily.

BUSINESS KEY CODE

As you consciously create yourself, you can rise above your past conditioning and past programming and decide which beliefs you desire to retain and which to release.

HOW TO FIX YOUR UNDERLYING ATTITUDES AND BELIEFS

Think about how you feel when you wake up, your mental state before you even get to work, and the attitude you carry with you. Then, think about starting the day with a positive mindset, looking forward to the workday, feeling the wonderful business opportunities that will unfold throughout the day and the supportive and trustworthy people you encounter. A short meditation, along with some positive affirmations, can help reverse your pessimistic thought process and propel you in the right direction during your interactions with all the people you come in contact with during the day.

Start each day by saying to yourself, "I know today will be a successful day. I will encounter the right people and be presented with incredible opportunities." Or, "I know my work is valued and recognized by the right people, and I am honored for my efforts." After saying your affirmations, take a few minutes to put yourself in a relaxed state of quiet meditation. This can include finding a tranquil place in your mind, free from fears and distractions, then visualizing your workday going well and your affirmations coming to fruition. Saying a few affirmations and then meditating should take only ten minutes. If you are always in a rush in the morning, you might need to change your alarm clock and wake up ten minutes earlier every day. Those ten minutes can always be wisely spent shifting your mental beliefs to transform your work life!

The second thing you need to do is stay in that mindset when you go out and interact with people throughout your day. This is especially important to keep in mind when encountering difficult or even toxic people directing their negative energy toward you. If you can remain calm, relaxed, and positive, the other person will have difficulty keeping up their negative energy. If you do find yourself slipping back into a negative mindset when dealing with negative people, imagine yourself flowing positive and heartfelt energy from your being toward the other person. We are spiritual beings, and our attitudes toward each other have a powerful effect on our interactions. You can send out this positive energy in advance during your morning meditation if you know you will be encountering a negative person at work or during the day.

Another method to foster positive relationships in the workplace and in your personal life is "positive communication." Perhaps you are shy and afraid of confrontation or tend toward more aggressive and angry communication. To avoid these pitfalls, focus on how you communicate with others. Make sure you keep a positive attitude and direct positive energy toward the other person in every interaction. Practicing open and positive communication can help build or repair bridges between coworkers, clients, bosses, employees, and personal relationships. If you lack in this area or are challenged by interacting with others, watch videos online of people with a frequency you aspire to, or better yet, interact with them. Positive communication is a great resource you can comprehend, drawing from many sources to master it quickly.

HOW DO WE CREATE A WINNING ATTITUDE AT WORK?

A winning attitude improves relationships and manifests promotions and opportunities. It increases sales and production and creates improvements in all areas of your work. But how do we maintain the positive mentality necessary for going through life with a winning attitude?

READY, SET, TAKE ACTION

What is your vision for life? Without vision, we can feel lost. No matter what appears to be happening in your business or personal life, visualize your life filled with passion and purpose. Take the time each day to appreciate the business process—and don't forget to have fun.

1. Manifest a winning attitude by replacing negative responses to external stimuli with positive responses.
2. Change the dialogue you internalize daily as you encounter situations and who may be working against you.
3. Develop higher personal standards, but be careful not to let your ego get inflated.
4. Try to be kind. Be the kind of person you wish to see in others. Lead, and they will follow.

Your mind is habitually drawn to negative beliefs, judgments, and expectations. So let's say, for example, someone else at your company gets a promotion you were hoping for. Your mind may immediately self-sabotage with thoughts like, "Of course I didn't get it. I'm just not smart enough," or "Good things never happen to me, so why would this be any different?" or "That person always gets ahead while I am stuck in this dead-end position."

If we could retrain our brains to respond oppositely, we would say things like, "Everything happens for a reason, and I know something better is coming my way," or "Now that I didn't receive that promotion or sale, I will self-evaluate to raise my frequency, improve my inner dialogue, and network with a higher caliber of individuals" or "Since the promotion did not solidify for me, I am going to evaluate if this is still a career path that I am passionate about. Perhaps I did not bring authentic inspiration to my career because I was no longer passionate."

BUSINESS KEY CODE

Clear your mind and understand every word you utter should positively influence you, those around you, and your inner thoughts. Fine-tune your vocabulary! Give your mind a break by eliminating all negative thoughts and expressions.

People respond easily to your inspiration and drive. As a result, your career grows. This is called divine-right timing. When your frequency aligns with your highest value of yourself and your work, the money and the clients will arrive, along with an abundance of miracles. The key is to remain non-judging and noncritical yet open and communicative.

Positive responses bring strong solutions. When you respond to adversity negatively, you kick off an emotional downward spiral in which you keep attracting more negative events. You can begin by asking what-if? questions.

❀ "What if I get an even better promotion next week?"
❀ "What if I obtain a raise and some praise for my efforts from my new boss?"
❀ "What if I become really focused on what I am passionate about and discover that I am truly inspired by a completely different career where I excel and feel elated?"

When we start looking at each moment of our lives as though everything happens for a reason and then respond with positive solutions to the challenges we encounter, our luck can turn around for us in a magical way. Making this a daily habit also helps to continue the growth cycle toward the improvement of becoming happy within ourselves.

READY, SET, TAKE ACTION

These are some self-care exercises to take stock in your life and create your own space of clarity and daily purpose.

1. Be aware of your thoughts, words, and actions. The universe will respond to what you tell yourself daily.
2. Continue your internal conversations with positive language like, "I can do it," "I can succeed," and "I know my life is extraordinary. I can upgrade and improve even more if I just change my attitude and mindset."

3. Have faith that your career, relationships, and life can transform at any time and age, as long as you commit to positivity.

4. Take a "thank-you" walk every morning. This walk is focused on improving your mood and clarifying your mind. Focus on your gratitude during this time rather than stressing about whatever you feel you lack.

After clarifying your passions and desires in life, take measures to move forward with this newfound sense of clarity. Whether this means changing careers or focusing on a new promotion, be clear on your goals, intentions, and desires to work toward making your blueprint into a reality. You can begin by participating in educational business seminars, self-realization workshops, business coaching, strategy conferences, mentoring programs, online videos, written books or audiobooks, and documentaries or educational films. Always continue to improve yourself, and you will continue to transform your life positively. It is cause and effect; every learning completion is the beginning of an exciting new opportunity.

BUSINESS KEY CODE

Obstacles present us with opportunities. Depending on how we view our experiences, we can grow from them.

You have the power to accomplish so much more as an individual or as a business team player. To envision your future, you must begin to live that future in your present life. Remember: what you give out is what comes back to you. You emanate and believe what you will receive, so align yourself with the frequency you desire to attract. You must continue to manifest and spread peace, love, joy, and harmony as you bring your whole self to the business world.

DAILY EMPOWERMENT AFFIRMATION

"I know today will be a successful day. I will encounter the right people and be presented with incredible opportunities."

THE WRAP-UP:
ALL YOU NEED TO KNOW

- ❀ Examine your limiting beliefs. Eliminate any misconceptions you have about success.
- ❀ Continue to open your heart as you tear down the walls you use to keep out from pain and disappointment.
- ❀ Take time to be present today.
- ❀ Actively seek to collaborate with a specific purpose, and work with people who have skills or talents you lack.
- ❀ Use positive communication. Make sure that in every interaction, you keep a positive attitude and direct positive energy toward the other person.
- ❀ Start trying to figure out what reignites your passion for life, and pursue that.
- ❀ The key to success is to stop focusing on others and start focusing on yourself.

CHAPTER
10

❁

THE INTENTION PRINCIPLE

E very single being, event, movement, relationship, and opportunity starts with the seed of intention. Intentions are powerful thoughts that take place on a plane of higher consciousness. What does that mean? Your thoughts have true strength, and your intentions can be used to raise your consciousness and align with a higher purpose for your life. Once you know this, it is up to you to become keenly aware of your ownership and responsibility for each thought sent out into the world. Harnessing the power of creating energy and success will lead to new-found respect from peers and family. Ultimately, focusing on the power of intention will help you to manifest a more purpose-driven life. You are your thoughts, and thus, you are the architect of your reality.

ALIGNING WITH THE UNIVERSE

If it is true that your current reality is a direct result of your thoughts and feelings, and you want to change the current state of events, how do you go about bringing transformation? Why is it, you might ask, that you continue to struggle in certain areas that you have hoped to change? Maybe you desire a higher-paying career but you ignore the fact that, at the moment, you live beyond your means, which keeps you in a state of surviving from paycheck to paycheck. When you are in your authentic self, you do not need to prove anything through status, materialistic, or ego-based intentions.

As you send out thoughts into the world, each vibrates at a unique frequency. It's a simple but difficult process, but the reality is that the energy you send out is the same energy you are bound to receive. In other words, when you desire abundance, you must avoid discouraging statements like, "My future is insecure, my livelihood is in danger, and scarcity is rampant," or "I never seem to get far enough ahead to stop the anxiety and fear," or "All the money in the world can't make me happy. Life is just working against me no matter what."

Yes, we all need money to survive, but you must balance it with love and health to bring yourself into a state of authentic oneness in all areas of your spiritual and business life. Negative intentions can sabotage the biggest dreams and desires, even for the most deserving individuals. Remember, you are your thoughts, and that includes thoughts about the world, yourself, and others. When you arrive at this realization and you become responsible for every intention you hold, you will become laser-focused on emitting only positive intentions. You will raise your energy frequency, and the results will bring your dreams into reality.

BUSINESS KEY CODE

Whatever you want and need, you already have. It is available to you. You just need to claim it. Just say *yes*.

OVERCOMING OBSTACLES

You will begin to attract more of what you want by sending out the "new" intentions. If you lack wealth or opportunity, you will likely continuously face obstacles to your success. If this makes you feel frustrated, discouraged, or frightened, there is still an internal belief that "lack" has a place in your life. And beware, if you focus only on what you can obtain, never thinking of service or giving back to others, you may finally obtain what you desire, only to have it taken away by the universe. Focusing solely on what you can get from the universe based on fear, greed, or selfishness is still affirming lack. Truly wealthy individuals don't focus on lack because they see a limitless pool of abundance in the world that everyone can share.

READY, SET, TAKE ACTION

A fear of being powerful often keeps people damaged and powerless. Look beneath the surface and into the cause, and you will discover what has held you back. Practice looking at all situations and qualities of your life, and be aware of your purposes, goals, wants, and dreams.

1. Put down the fear. Whatever encumbrances you are carrying, put them down for a moment and rest. They will still be there after you are rested and more powerful.
2. Seek to collaborate with a specific purpose. Work with people who have unique and diverse skills.
3. Spend more time with positive people. If there is someone you know who is happy and engaging, invite them to an activity that you can both enjoy.
4. Get it done today. Avoidance means not facing up to something that's bothering you. When you have unresolved issues, such as fear or anxiety, you may end up procrastinating important work or deadlines.

This will help align you with the mindset of powerful belief in yourself, clearing away all doubts and fears. Breaking old patterns, beliefs, and agreements is necessary to create ultimate freedom and release the past. Through this, new confidence springs from within. This confidence is necessary because everyone encounters daunting obstacles that block their path to a brighter future. The good news is that you can always fall back on the basics of the intention principle. If you learn to become very disciplined in your thought patterns, you will send out only thoughts of positivity and determination. You will manifest abundance from intention, just like having a direct line to the universe. Each challenge is a lesson and an opportunity to own more of ourselves. You have power over the reality you exist within. The obstacles you face are not as real as you believe; they are temporary limitations that your mind has accepted as permanent. Solutions are born from your burning desire to solve the problem and the clear knowledge of what you wish for. The conditions of your life right now result from decisions you made in the past, so if you want to change your future, you need to be authentic and trust yourself and the process and live every day in gratitude.

BUSINESS KEY CODE

Make your mind work for you instead of against you by adjusting your attitude, perception, and confidence.

STEPS TO ATTRACTING WHAT YOU WANT

As you improve your ability to put out strong intentions, you may begin to direct the course of your life to attract the very people, opportunities, jobs, and events you desire. The challenge will be to stay in positive alignment with your set intention. Below are some practical steps to help you accomplish that.

STEP 1: HOW TO SET AN INTENTION

Example: You set an intention to have a business marketing career in two years. Fantastic! Go get it! You set goals and take action. You brush up on your marketing, communication, and technology skills. You attend networking events and send relevant employers your resume—all great first steps.

STEP 2: USING AFFIRMATIONS AND DAILY INTENTIONS

Example: Hold on to that intention, and affirm your desire daily. Every day, say things like, "I have a fulfilling and prosperous business marketing career that I love." The key is in the repetition.

STEP 3: STAYING IN ALIGNMENT

How? As you achieve your goal, pay close attention to your thought patterns and what you say aloud. Every time you speak, think, or decide something, ask yourself, "Do my thoughts, words, and actions align with my ultimate purpose?" Your heart and your intuition will answer that question. Open your awareness, and you will feel the energy. If you feel uncomfortable, you probably need to rethink your decisions or reaffirm positivity in your thought patterns.

STEP 4: STAYING OPEN AND DETACHED

How? Avoid hyper-focusing on the outcome or result. Instead, fixate on staying in alignment. If you align with the universe and all it can give you, a new life of happiness will unfold in front of you. You will eventually create just about anything you desire, but for now, you must stay open and detached. In other words, set the intention and then witness how the universe delivers it in miraculous ways. Don't get attached to a belief that your path to success will be exactly how you imagined it because the universe has a higher supply of creativity for you to experience. This is where you must trust the process and trust yourself to stay in alignment. Stay open and detached, and the universe will educate and reward you. You will manifest the business clients, individuals, and situations that create these opportunities.

BUSINESS KEY CODE

We need to honor life, realizing it is a great gift that we get to shape and mold into what we wish it to become.

PERSISTENCE CREATES RESULTS

It is so easy to lose motivation and quickly give up after beginning the journey to success. You must realize now that it is not enough to obtain motivation if you cannot stay in that frequency of determination. When you remain motivated, persistence is the basis of your continued movement toward your objective. See everything through to the end, and get used to doing that. Start with small, simple goals so you can proceed to achieving and finalizing your tasks. After you have accomplished some less intimidating goals, relish in the achievement. Feel yourself being successful! As you become accustomed to success, your more impressive goals will become less daunting. Surround yourself with like-minded people who will support your projects and your talents. Build networks of people who will contribute to your ongoing success. Commit to being motivated because whatever you are committed to will generate results and move you in the direction of incredible miracles.

THE FLOW OF INFINITE POTENTIAL

Sometimes, no matter how hard we focus on being positive, our path can still become discouraging. When you inevitably encounter challenges on the road to success, then make sure not to regress into a previous, negative mode of operation. Instead, make a different choice to reaffirm that you remain faithful and you will manifest the best life experience. Return to a frequency of trust and optimism. Allow yourself to be appreciated and respected, and know you are a fully functional, whole person who attracts positivity. Desire not to control others but rather to have confidence in your creative process. Through this, you will raise your frequency and begin to radiate your authentic presence, which will create more success within your business and yourself.

Here is where the intention principle displays its true value. Staying in a mode of "want" can leave you feeling anxious and depleted. Instead, reverse your thought process. If you desire abundant connections and wealth, you should send out that intention to receive it back. But how can you emanate abundance, especially when you are coming from a place of fear and anxiety? You must discontinue your belief that your reality is plagued by scarcity and start truly believing that abundance is now commonplace in your life. Trust yourself to utilize the intention principle and truly believe it to receive it.

Imagine for a minute your circumstances suddenly changed and you had everything you desired. In an instant, you would be content, satisfied, and well-situated to give back to the world and the people around you. Today you should radiate the energy from that intention, even if you haven't yet obtained what you envisioned. Don't wait for your circumstances to change before changing your thoughts and feelings. You have the strength to accomplish so much more as an individual or team player. To envision your future, you must begin to live that future in your present life. Remember, the energy you emit is the result you attract. Stay authentic in your interactions with yourself and others to always have something valuable to share. Love, respect, and integrity are the keys to a positive, happy life.

GET READY TO LIVE

A life and work balance doesn't have to be complex, dramatic, or chaotic. You just need to be a team player and utilize accountability, integrity, and gratitude in all functions of yourself and your business. Remember that your life is full of meaning and purpose but also that you need to maximize the scope of your potential. Stay compassionate with yourself and with all others while you are still learning from your experiences. Choose to be around people you admire and respect and who align with your highest values and intentions. Create integrity by staying true to the habits and thoughts that bring balance to your life and work.

Finding your authentic self is a process of opening up and uncovering your unique form of expression. If you honor and embrace your individual power, you will fully discover the potential for unlimited possibilities in your life. Don't internalize any negative energy or feelings of anxiety for any reason, and examine everything that you think and feel using a positive mindset. This will allow you to go deeper into your consciousness and uncover the origin and strength of your authentic self. If you view life as working against you while reaffirming to yourself that you lack the ability to succeed, then you can be left feeling empty, afraid, and hopeless. You must pay close attention to your thoughts and actions throughout each day to remain hopeful and strong in the face of adversity.

The authentic self is alive within each of us. You possess all the power necessary to bring balance and success into your work and personal life and manifest any intention into reality. Your path may not take shape exactly how you envisioned it, but the results may be more impressive than anything you had ever imagined.

You possess infinite potential through your ability to make any intention part of your reality. This potential is realized only when you leave behind all the fears and anxieties about the future that have kept you paralyzed for so long. Without a vision or strong intention, there will be no remarkable future because the future is created by our hearts, minds, and will. Each moment is an opportunity to be at the forefront of something new and exciting. There are no accidents, and your daily interactions must be something you have confidence in. You design the future with your desires. Learn to trust yourself now so all your actions going forward will always unify you with your highest values and goals. Every situation, person, and event is brought to you because it is in your best interest to learn the lessons that life has prepared for you. By releasing and not acknowledging the fear of the unknown, you can create an extraordinary, successful, abundantly happy, and inspired life. Right now, I give you permission and encourage you to go out and live life to its fullest extent.

DAILY EMPOWERMENT AFFIRMATION

I choose to live honestly and compassionately with integrity.

The Wrap-Up:
All You Need to Know

- ✿ Do something every day that is related to your goal and moves you in that direction.
- ✿ Start each morning with a fresh new positive affirmation.
- ✿ A life and work balance doesn't have to be difficult or chaotic; you just need to stay in a mindset of accountability, integrity, and gratitude in all your personal and business endeavors.
- ✿ When you encounter overwhelming obstacles along the road to success, remember not to fall back into past negative behaviors.
- ✿ If you need support or expertise, get someone to help you along the way.
- ✿ Align with your inner self and master the learning process that leads you to your next growth experience.
- ✿ Discovering your authentic self is a process of seeking your inner voice and uncovering your unique form of expression.
- ✿ All obstacles and challenges present opportunities for improvement.
- ✿ Commit to staying in a state of motivation. Whatever you are committed to will generate results and move you in the direction of incredible miracles.

AFTERWORD

Become Your Own Business Guru is a compilation of knowledge that I felt needed to be shared during these challenging times. Through any crisis, challenge, or breakdown, we are all creating a frequency shift that is an alignment of our inner selves with our best version of ourselves. By staying persistent and patient, you will have long-lasting success and fulfillment in all aspects of your life and business. The commitment to your happiness and the process of change is the key to seeing your life begin to truly evolve. Keeping your thoughts, words, and actions in a positive state of mind will cause your life to reflect your intention. Staying positive can often help you overcome many tough challenges and embrace change. No one does anything alone. Every successful endeavor involves the contributions of many individuals.

I have created and manifested wonderful experiences with brilliant individuals that have taught me how to practice well-being, focus my intent, and remain in a place of happiness and positivity no matter what. Now is the best time to take an honest look within yourself because you'll discover exactly what you need to find. You are now ready to approach life and business with newfound accountability and authenticity. You must remember that you can be anything, do anything, and have anything you desire as long as you dare to stay on your path and call forth the wisdom, love, and strength you possess within yourself.

ACKNOWLEDGMENTS

Thank you, Sylvia Hayse, of the Hayse Literary Agency, LLC, for your dedication and hard work.

Thank you, Greg McKay, for your professional help and expertise in editing. Your input and brilliant skills are so appreciated.

Thank you, Patricia, Doriana Mazzola, Sante Losio, Gina McKay, Diane Robin, Ute Ville, Catherine Carlin, Debra Johnston, Cozette Dunlap, Laurie D. Muslow, Ilyce Glink, Tony Sweet, Victoria Cordova, Bruce R. Hatton, Keith Cohn of CCreative Design, Robert Tauler, and David Bailey, for your insight and support.

A heartfelt thanks to Evelyn M. Dalton for your unwavering belief, dedication, and all-embracing love that is with me each day of my life.

Thank you to my worldwide team of event organizers and promoters.

A very special thanks to all my clients who have supported all my work over the years.

RECOMMENDED READING

Braden, Gregg. *The Wisdom Codes*. Carlsbad: Hay House, 2020.

Moorjani, Anita. *Sensitive Is the New Strong*. New York: Atria/Simon and Schuster, 2021.

Duhigg, Charles. *The Power of Habit*. New York: Random House, 2019.

Housel, Morgan. *The Psychology of Money*. UK: Harriman House, 2020.

Bandler, Richard. *How to Take Charge of Your Life*: *The User's Guide to NLP*. Harper Collins, 2014.

Hoodyar, Tom—Dotz, Tom—Sanders, Susan. *NLP: The Essential Guide to Neuro-Linguistic Programming*. William Morrow, 2013.

Hignon, Ray and Jessica. *Time, Money, Freedom*. Hay House, 2020.

Nestor, James. *Breath*. New York: Riverhead Penguin Books, 2020.

Singer, Michael. *The Untethered Soul*. Harbinger/Noetic Publications, 2007.

Mark Nepo. *The Book Of Awakening*. Conari Press, 2000.

Achor, Shawn. *The Happiness Advantage.* New York: Crown Business, 2010.

Amen, D. G. *Change Your Brain, Change Your Life.* New York: Three Rivers Press, 1998.

Covey, Stephen. The 7 Habits of Highly Effective People—*Anniversary Edition.* Simon and Schuster, 2020.

Lipton, Bruce. *The Biology of Belief: Unleashing the Power of Consciousness, Matter, & Miracles.* Carlsbad: Hay House, 2008.

Di Martini, John. *Inspired Destiny.* Carlsbad: Hay House, 2010.

ABOUT THE AUTHOR

International motivational speaker, life coach, intuitive strategist, and best-selling author Gary Quinn shares his valuable insights and knowledge with a worldwide audience via his self-help inspirational books, podcasts, television appearances, online digital downloads, and numerous worldwide speaking engagements and seminars. Gary Quinn is the host of *Ready Set Live*, a popular personal development, lifestyle, and wellness podcast.

His teachings have been embraced by people from all walks of life, including entertainers, athletes, and corporate leaders. Among his many clients are Academy Award winners, Grammy winners, and Olympic gold medalists. His corporate clients include CEOs, vice presidents, fashion designers, marketing directors, and executives from many international companies. He has worked with individuals and business groups from Coldwell Banker Global Luxury, HP Hauser Partners Legal Services, Tauler Smith LLP, Irinox SpA, Amazon, Indigo Payments, D.D. Dunlap Companies Inc., Shiseido Japan, Microsoft, DHL, and Della Volpe & Partners.

Gary is in demand worldwide for seminars, corporate events, and private sessions. He frequently holds retreats and seminars in the United States, Switzerland, England, Japan, Ireland, Italy, Austria, Germany, Mexico, and Canada.

Gary has been featured in *Vogue, Huffington Post, Psychology Today, Glamour, Gala, Toronto Sun, Woman's Weekly, Red Magazine, YOGA Magazine, People Magazine, Us Weekly, Reader's Digest,* and *InStyle*. He has appeared on Extra TV, NBC, FOX, BBC, ITV, Rai TV, RTÉ Television Ireland, Mediaset Italy, and more than 150 worldwide radio broadcasts.

TOUCHSTONE FOR LIFE
COACHING PROGRAM©

Gary Quinn is the founder of the Touchstone for Life Coaching Certification Program©, which trains and transforms individuals to create successful results in their lives.

The coaching program is intended to help individuals maximize their potential and achieve peak performance, evident in both personal life and business acumen.

Gary Quinn's certified coaching will help you strategize and create a blueprint for success. He offers seminars, private coaching, keynote speaking, consulting, and training to become a certified Touchstone for Life Coach.

To receive a free monthly newsletter and more information, visit www.garyquinn.tv.

Join me on Instagram (@garyhquinn), LinkedIn (Gary Quinn), Facebook (Gary Quinn), and Twitter (@garyhquinn).

Touchstone for Life Coaching Program©
P.O. Box 16041 Beverly Hills, California 90209 USA

PGIL2023USA